AF375277

Hello
My Name is
"Sober"

Breaking the Silence of
Alcoholism, &
How to Live in Sobriety

Anthony Torres

To my beautiful wife Sasha, Thank you for not giving up on me. But most importantly, thank you for not giving up on US.

This Book is Dedicated to all the people who lost
their lives to Alcoholism. Be at Peace now
#Breakthesilence
#togethorwecan
#Sober

Contents

Chapter 1

Hi, my name is "Anthony"

To lose yourself in Alcoholism is to find yourself in Sobriety. What's lost can always be found.

-Me

It was 5 am. My body was hunched over the floor and my face planted in the toilet, sick and weak from a full night of drinking. I had already been bingeing for days, and my body was now screaming that it'd had enough. With each forceful expulsion of vomit, I gripped my stomach in dread, fearing that my insides would implode from the pain. Once empty, I wiped the remaining vomit off my chin and wondered, "Why do I always get to this point in my life?" It was becoming increasingly obvious how much Alcoholism was destroying me.

I gathered enough strength to rise up and open the door, only to find my six-year-old daughter standing there, confused and concerned. My sickness had clearly unsettled her, as she'd been too afraid to enter the bathroom to see what was wrong with me. All she could do was wait and listen to her daddy's painful screams, unsure of what was happening or how to intervene. Not only was I realizing how much alcoholism had gotten the best of me; I was now coming face to face with its devastating effects and memories for my family.

It's one thing for this to happen when you're alone, but another much more painful thing to happen in the presence of your kids. And I can promise you that families feel every bit of suffering that we do; our pain becomes theirs' in time. And our Alcoholism will become a shadow draped over them. A shadow, that is hard for them to escape from. Alcoholism in families has damaged more kids emotionally then we can imagine, it has tugged at the heart strings of kids for centuries. I certainly never envisioned this situation for myself or my family, yet I reached a place I'd never thought I'd reach and had crossed the line of "Losing Control."

From the tender age of 14, all I knew was that I was a drinker. I was never the type of person that could have just one and be done. Once that cold drink touched my mouth, I was fully committed. I was going to drink till I got drunk and I was not going to apologize for it—even if it meant days of bingeing, not knowing where I'd end up; even if it meant getting behind the wheel of a vehicle; even if it meant going to jail or losing my own life. All I can say is this: I was a ball rolling down a hill, and I didn't know when or even if this ride would end. Before I knew it, years had gone by—same old story, same old dance.

The saddest part about my drinking was that I'd brought my family along for the ride—a ride that they definitely did not sign up for. And this was not your typical Brady Bunch or any other fictional TV family. This was their reality: a dad who drank—a dad who made promises he couldn't keep. Meanwhile, from my point of view, I was a prized package, and my drinking was simply a part of me, like a measly quirk or character flaw. What you saw was what you got.

I tend to see this pattern much more in Hispanic culture: the husband is a drinker, and the wife feels stuck or obligated to stay and endure the chaos. No matter how difficult things get, she remains steadfast, tirelessly attending to the family's needs while putting her own on the backburner. Should the thought to leave ever cross her mind, she would remember those vows, "For Better or for Worse", or perhaps consider how much time she'd already invested into the relationship. Whatever the case, some of them stay; there is no doubt that marriages can survive Alcoholism. Though, the way I see it, something has to give: the relationship or the drinking. The real question is, "How much are people willing to sacrifice?"

As I type this, I wonder how many women have put their lives and dreams on hold to care for their alcoholic husbands. They look in the mirror and ask, "How much more can I give? How much longer can I go on?"

This was my wife, Sasha, thirteen years ago. She had given and gone through so much to keep our family together. After clinging to our relationship as long as she possibly could, one day, it was time for her to let me go. By this point, my Alcoholism had cast a long shadow over my family, blinding me to everything else. Drinking and going out with my friends outweighed the presence of those awaiting me at home. No one wakes up thinking "Today, I will be an Alcoholic"; over time, it just happens, and once you realize it, it's too late. Over time, what begins as an innocent social engagement, soon becomes our sole means of functioning.

Personally, I felt like it was just what men did. If we were at a function, we drank; if we were at a ball game, we drank; if we grilled, we drank; if we were in the comfort of our own homes and felt like having a beer, we drank (with no more hesitation than if we wanted a Dr. Pepper). But when does it become a problem for us?

I think drinking becomes a problem when we lose control of our true selves—when we put it before the people we love, can't operate without it, have to lie and deceive just to get it, or we don't even see how it's affecting our relationships.

As I reflect on my life, I can recall several instances when I thought I had control but didn't—when I would tell myself "Oh, I will never be like that" or "those who can't control their alcohol are weak." Yet, there I was, gradually losing control of my own life.

I'll never forget the breaking point that triggered my recovery. Sasha eventually got fed up with my drinking, lies, and late nights. Without any notice, she took the kids and left me, and I finally had to make a choice: get Sober or continue to drink until, sooner or later, I lost my own life. For months, I continued to drink, unwilling to face reality or the burden of regaining control. Though, as consequences grew larger, I eventually choose Sobriety, which redeemed my family's trust and helped me find my purpose in life. Today, I'm just thankful I survived to share my story. Today, I am thankful that, in time, my family healed.

Throughout this book, I will share bits and pieces of my life, as well as measures I've taken to recover from Alcoholism. Everyone's story is different, but we all have one thing in common: we're all on this journey together. If you're reading these words right now, you want to get better. Whether this is your step 1 or step 100, recovery is not a solo journey; we're a community bound by the shared hope for a healthier, brighter future.

I write this book out of the ashes but also out of pain— the residual pain and damage that comes with being an Alcoholic. I also write out of sorrow for those who've lost and are losing the battle to Alcoholism—for so many families destroyed. I truly believe we don't talk about it enough. We don't expose the harsh truths that need to be spoken. If this book could help just one person, one family, then it's done its job. I am no better than anyone else; I am just someone who made it. And now, my mission is to help as many people as possible.

Hi, my name is Anthony Torres, and today, I am 13 years sober. If I can do it, so can you.

Consider me your friend as we process through these crucial discussions on Alcoholism and what we can do to stop it, so that, by the end of this book, you too can say, "Hi, my name is _______, and I am Sober. I have stopped drinking; I have stopped causing myself and my family pain; I have changed the trajectory of my family for the better." This book is designed to aid and spark thought, perhaps helping you heal at least some areas of your life in the process. Though, my hope is that, ultimately, it shows you how important you are—how much we need you more than the drinking does.

Take a moment to imagine what this would look like for you—what a clean and Sober life would look like for your family years down the line.

And keep this in mind as we go through this book: we don't have to blend in with society to be accepted. We need bold men and women that choose to be different, because this journey of Sobriety requires courage and a willingness to break the cycle. When everyone in your environment is screaming at you "YES," you have to be strong enough to put up boundaries and say "no." Social acceptance is not always in your best interest, so sometimes the only way to truly help those around you is by taking the necessary steps to help yourself first.

Living a Sober life is one of the greatest gifts I could've given myself, and I wish I could've experienced it sooner. But life is all about living and learning. The lower you go, the higher you can rise. I hope this book inspires you to give that gift to yourself—to rise a little higher, one day at a time. As we move through this journey together, let's embrace the promise that each sober day brings—a promise of personal growth, resilience, and the rediscovery of life's boundless joys. Until we see that Alcoholism has become a problem in our family's history and even ourselves. It will continue to be a problem.

Chapter 2

The Origins of Alcoholism & Where We Are Today

> *"Because alcohol is encouraged by our culture, we get the idea that it isn't dangerous. However, alcohol is the most potent and most toxic."*
> -Beverly A. Potter

When we think of Alcoholism, we often consider it a modern day engagement. Though, in reality, it's been around for ages. Back then, there were no overall solutions to the major health challenges people faced, resulting in numerous fatalities due to liver and heart failure. There was also no clear association between alcohol and the number of failed marriages, with so many broken and damaged lives left behind in the process. Little did they know, the alcohol was altering their emotions—altering how they thought and, ultimately, altering their lives. I'm reminded of that drinking culture every time I watch an old movie like "Tombstone" or "Titanic"—portrayals of real life back then as it unfortunately still is today. Though, the late-night-partiers and all-out-drinkers from the past were much less aware of the consequences behind their actions (whereas now, we have less excuses).

In the distant past, across ancient civilizations from Japan to Greece, mankind experimented with the fermentation of fruits and grains, giving rise to this unique drink—a drink that altered the brain, making you feel a certain way. As the first sip of Alcohol was consumed, by earliest account, around 7000 BC, I believe our world was changed forever (9,000 years of sipping: The history of alcoholism, 2020).

According to Wikipedia, this drink was offered in Egypt to those who faced death or depression as a means to escape their sorrows. Does this sound familiar? How many times have you heard people say, "I drink to not feel anymore," "I drink to let loose," or, even more commonly, "I drink to take the edge off." Today, we find ourselves unable to confront our emotions without relying on the crutch of Alcohol, so much so that we've convinced ourselves it's a safe and healthy option. And this pattern has carried on for centuries. From our ancestors' first sip, the seeds of Alcoholism were sown, setting a destructive cycle into motion that has extended over into generations and is still in full swing today. Whether we can or even want to stop it often remains uncertain. Sometimes I sit and wonder if we even want the cycle to stop.

But I'm here to tell you that we can! And that's the whole purpose of this book—to break the silence surrounding this generational killer that's wreaked havoc on our families for decades. And breaking this vicious cycle starts with you. By gathering the strength and discipline to say NO to Alcohol, our families can begin the process of healing and restoration so we can finally see a new generation of healthy, sober individuals. My heartfelt hope is for people to realize their dreams and goals without the temptation to the destructive grip of Alcoholism. Let's eliminate the stigma that labels entire families as "Alcoholics" and replace it with hope—a tangible, believable, achievable goal of making Sobriety a reality. Alcoholism has robbed families and individuals of their peace, joy, and potential for far too long. It's time to fight back and reclaim all that was lost and more!

Consider how many marriages fail due to Alcoholism—how many marriages never even had a chance because alcohol got mixed in with the Vows? Half of all marriages end in divorce, and according to Gitnux's Market Data 2023 Report, approximately 50% of those divorced couples cite alcohol abuse as a leading factor.

I also wonder how many deaths and prison sentences could've been avoided if alcohol wasn't in the picture. I receive countless letters from inmates about their failed relationships, poor choices, and lives derailed by alcohol. Through my prison ministry, I constantly hear men and women declare, "If only I'd gotten help with my drinking sooner" or "I've been drinking for so long; it's all I know."

Every bad habit has a root in our lives, and once we identify that root, we must wield an axe and strike at it immediately, severing those ties for good. By cutting ourselves off from the source of Alcoholism, the generational destruction naturally begins to fade. Your family line has been eagerly awaiting someone like you—someone with enough courage and boldness to step forward and confidently strike at that root once and for all.

Vincent van Gogh, recognized both for his artistic brilliance and his penchant for alcohol, is speculated by some to have turned to drinking for his schizophrenia. Nevertheless, at the age of 37, he tragically took his own life (9,000 years of sipping: The history of alcoholism, 2020). The question lingers: was alcohol a contributing factor, enabling him to make such a devastating decision? While we'll never know for sure, I certainly believe it's likely. Just think about how many times you've awakened with regret or guilt tied to actions influenced by alcohol. The only difference in Van Gogh's case, along with the cases of many others, is that the consequences are irreversible—there's no chance of recovery or amends. One can't help but wonder how much more art we could've enjoyed if Van Gogh had never picked up the bottle. And I can't help but wonder how many gifts the world would miss from you if alcohol were to overshadow your brightness and purpose.

Needless to say, I've experienced my fair share of Alcoholism. There were numerous days spent at the bar, showing up when it opened and staying out till it closed. Blackouts were frequent, leaving me wondering to what I'd said or done, followed by many mornings of sickness and regret. There were even moments when I sat alone in the darkness, holding a gun to my temple and contemplating if I should stay or go. That fierce internal battle, complicated by mixed sensations of pain, sorrow, anger, fear, confusion, doubt, and altered brain chemistry creates a trap that feels outright inescapable—a trap I wouldn't wish upon my worst enemy.

Once again, I reflect on how much drama I could have spared my family—how many nights I could've granted my kids peace instead of chaos and security instead of uncertainty. I ponder how many nights they must have felt uneasy, wondering if I was coming home—if Sasha and I would get into another heated shouting match.

Understanding the impact of Alcoholism on a family requires firsthand experience. The emotional damage it inflicts is only truly grasped by those who've lived it. Every alcoholic with a family tends to believe their struggles are unique, yet in my counseling sessions, a clear pattern emerges: it's the same hurt, same cycle, same destruction, same pain. And the most heart-wrenching part about it is that our loved ones are powerless to stop us.

As a full-time minister with a growing circle of people familiar with my recovery ministry, I frequently receive calls to visit individuals in prison, extend support to those in rehab, and pray with those on the brink of losing their lives to Alcoholism.

One day, I got a call to see a young woman in hospice who was dying from liver cirrhosis. This particular encounter struck me emotionally. I arrived at the home to find her young kids surrounding her, tears streaming down their faces. Weak and thin, the woman couldn't vocal any words—only groans of pain as she touched her swollen, fluid-filled stomach. My heart sank in the presence of her loved ones as they witnessed her slow decline. At one point, I laid my hands on her to pray and could sense every bit of regret, suffering, and long-held anger she harbored.

After leaving the home, I looked her up on Facebook to see if she was someone I had ministered to in the past.

Upon finding her page, I could hardly believe the vibrant young woman in the picture was the same woman I'd just seen dying in that bed. Alcohol had completely sucked the life out of her, leaving nothing behind but pain, suffering, and death—a tragic legacy to pass down to her family. This is what Alcoholism does. She had hopes, dreams, and a life—all shattered because the bottle had gotten the best of her. Two weeks later, this 27-year-old was dead, and I saw Alcoholism for what it really was: a drink that robs people of their lives, from one generation to the next. It leads to questions like: what drove her to drink? What events shaped her life? And whose drinking habits did she observe in her youth?

Alcohol is a silent killer—a slow and steady life-claimer. Even as I type this, someone has just fallen into to its deathly grip. They lost the battle like many of their ancestors and family members did. Alcohol never discriminates based on race or financial status. It can poison the heart of any human, rich and poor alike.

According to the CDC, Alcoholism claims 380 lives every day. Deep down, we cannot be okay with this, yet it remains a topic lacking in sufficient awareness and education. The intent of this book is to help those who are ready to make a change—ready to start viewing reality through an untouched lens, address the long-suppressed pain and sorrow deep inside, and stop the dangerous progression of Alcoholism in its tracks.

Perhaps this book might even be mocked by those who feel in control of their alcohol. Though, I write this book for the bulk of us who don't possess that power. And I hope it acts as a life jacket for the drowning and a rescue boat for those lost at sea.

If you're reading this and believe you're beyond reach or repair, I want to reinforce that you are mistaken! It's never too late to bring peace to your family and change your life in a positive direction. Listen, are you breathing? As long as you have breath in you, there's always hope and room for change in your life.

The greatest regret we may carry in life is not putting in the work to at least try to stop drinking. We look up at this mountain and decide it's simply not worth the climb because our habits have carried us down for so long. The self-assurance that "drinking is in our DNA; it's in our bloodstream; it's just who we are," does nothing but form a self-fulfilling lie that prevents us from realizing our untapped inner strength.

It all starts with how we talk to ourselves, so here's a question to keep in mind: how badly do you really want to get sober? Since we naturally invest our efforts into what matters most, it's time to get crystal clear and intentional about your priorities in life. What do you need to start saying "yes" and "no" to more often? What kind of boundaries need to be put in place? The most important thing to welcome into your life right now is "yes" to help and guidance—"yes" to positive change. This journey can only begin once we determine it's a "no" to alcohol.

The dark shadow Alcoholism has cast over the world has endured long enough, taking far more than it gives. It's time to reverse that destructive pattern and usher in the light of Sobriety. Despite the many years Alcoholism has claimed, I firmly believe we can recover what's been lost and more.

https://www.shorelinerecoverycenter.com/9000-years-of-sipping-the-history-of-alcoholism/

https://www.cdc.gov/chronicdisease/resources/publications/factsheets/alcohol.htm

Chapter 3

My Personal Demon with Alcoholism

I can feel you standing over the bed looking at me—hating on me, baiting me, betraying me. Breathing threats, I would one day regret. Your sweat dripping on me, trying to destroy me. You won't set me free!

Will you?

I hate you, but I need you. No one gets me enough to put up with me, but it's us three. I think I will just sit under this tree and die.

Do you know what you do to me? I hate me, I draw from me, I hurt me, I bleed for thee.

Can you see? It's getting darker, and I hear other voices. I see demons with four faces, I'm reaching out to God in unholy places.

I'm drowning in these suicidal thoughts. You seem to be the boss. Can you take your finger off the trigger? I don't want this gun to go off, to die in my thoughts.

I know you want to kill me. But this drink keeps me happy. Even when I'm suicidal, this empty moment is most vital.

I'm tired and just want to stop. But who am I fooling? I'm breaking, my shackles remaining. What am I saying? No one cares that I'm fading.

When I run the other way, you chase me—to plague me, to shake me, enslave me.

You know I'm in a puddle of my depression, no hint of expression. It calls into question whether I'll make it through my transgression.

Anxiety, self-pity within me, for I know even today's not guaranteed.

I wonder if I will die this way.

Though, one day I will defeat you. One day I'll be renewed. Can't you hear me screaming, "I am DONE WITH YOU!"?

One day I'll be blessed to rest, not stressed or hard-pressed. I'll look back refreshed and say "I found my way out of this mess."

One day you won't keep me, own me, control me. Can we agree?

One day I'll be happy, joyful, hopeful, unafraid. At last, I'll think clearly. One day!

One day my family will want to be around me rather than sidestepping to avoid me. I am not knee-deep. One day!

But right now, you get the best of me. You don't want to see me free. I must release this demon—release the screaming. After 15 years, I know you're not one to reason.

Within my chest, a lion's den. I just need to know if I'll feel again. No pretense, I won't defend. Truth is, I need you in the end.

I can't get back yesterday, it's gray. What will they say as I slowly decay? I need to push you away, so I can get sober.

One day!

But today, I enjoy my demon. It revels in my bleeding—that I'm that heathen, weakened, beaten, sinking. Can't you hear my voice? It sounds defeated.

One day…

I will be Sober. "One day!" they say. I no longer want to be this way! To be honest, I'm tired of being the prey.

One day!

Chapter 4

Hi, my name is "Stuck"

"F-E-A-R has two meanings: 'Forget Everything And Run' or 'Face Everything And Rise.' The choice is yours." - Zig Ziglar

We all know the storyline well: "I want to stop drinking, but I just don't know how."

Many people have said this to me over the years. I've even said it myself when I was a drinker. But how can we envision a life of Sobriety when we've been drinking our whole lives? When our family and friends still drink and we see it everywhere we go—at every sports event, entertainment venue, and restaurant? It reminds me of that old movie by Bruce Lee called "Enter the Dragon." In the mirrors scene, no matter which way he turns or tries to go, there he is, his enemy lurking behind him somewhere. It's the same with our alcohol—it's always lurking in the background.

I wonder how many people feel stuck in this cycle. They get tired of trying to quit so they drink—tired of never seeing progress so they drink. Instead, all they can see is every failed marriage or relationship, every unfulfilled promise and attempt leading to discouragement and more drinking. Hear me out on this:

Don't let failure consume you. The hope of one day being sober should motivate you to keep trying.

Just because you feel stuck does not mean you're a failure. I know that's what you feel, because I have felt it too. However, that feeling does not define you, it's only a result of your current circumstance. I want you to get this in your mind:

People don't stay stuck. They *choose* to.

That's right! You have a choice today and every day to get unstuck. I don't care how many times you have tried, fallen, or been in and out of rehab, NA, or AA. What matters is the choice you make right now to free yourself and keep trying until you do, because one day you will.

Facing the dread of a relapse was very difficult for me. Though, even in the midst of my slip-ups, I found gratitude in opening my eyes the next day, because I knew I had another opportunity to start all over again. Regardless of the challenges, I was determined to keep trying. While guilt and shame weigh heavy on the soul, so does stagnation and listening to the noise around us. It sure is a drag when we're trying to better ourselves and hear comments like, "I knew you couldn't do it," "I knew it was just a matter of time before you drank again," or, my favorite, "You will never change."

Believe it or not, those words fueled me! Not only did I want to prove those people wrong, I wanted to prove myself right. I wanted a new life—a new sober reason for living, not for anyone but myself.

I had finally reached a point where I was more tired of hurting myself and, most importantly, those around me, than I was tired of my repeated attempts and failures.

Fully aware of what I had become, the opinions of others didn't bother me. And you shouldn't let them bother you either. Here's a piece of advice I strongly encourage: Less talk, more do!

I can't even count how many times I used to say, "Today I am going to get sober," and by the end of the day, was drunk. So once I officially committed to my recovery, I didn't announce my intentions. I just did what I needed to do and pushed through. I went to church and my classes and kept myself busy. And If I relapsed, I didn't tell anyone either. I just picked myself up and kept going! Next thing you know, weeks, months, and eventually, one year had passed without a sip of alcohol.

I want to share a few key practices with you. They're simple things I still to do today.

First, recognize this: **Sober life = disciplined life.**

When people return to the bottle, it's because they lack discipline. Establishing a routine has been a game changer in my journey. Every morning, I drink my coffee and read my scripture. Now, it's simply who I am and what I do. I also try to eat right, go to the gym, get to bed by a certain time (because, according to my kids, I'm old), and find ways to make this world a little better. One way I do this is by sharing daily devotions and words of encouragement on social media.

This consistent self-care routine is crucial for relaxation and stress-relief, acting as a preventative measure from relying on alcohol for the same effect. While my life in recovery isn't flawless, I view it as generally disciplined. I am where I need to be and recognize that I must remain alert, because I know how easy it is to slip right back into drinking. And I've come way too far to go back.

Now, this doesn't mean I'm in drill sergeant mode 24/7. Some days, I just need to flop on the couch and do nothing. We all need breaks from time to time and shouldn't beat ourselves up over it. The key is simply to discover what works for you, and establish a routine based on your unique priorities. Once you find that discipline, you will find your strength for recovery.

There are 2 main areas of discipline:

1. You must be disciplined in your **surroundings.**

Let me ask you this: how important is your Sobriety? You're probably saying, "It's very important." Okay great! I am glad we are on the same page for this next part:

You have to be okay with losing family members and close friends for the sake of your Sobriety! Don't believe me? Stop going to BBQs and any family gathering where drinking is present and see what happens. Refrain from stepping foot in any area you used to drink (yes, even restaurants). I didn't go to Texas Roadhouse for two years for this reason. But let's take it even further. Your home—your place of peace and safety—should no longer be a nightly pub for your friends and family. Set a rule that anyone who comes over is not allowed to drink. This shift can be quite the shock, revealing who actually respects your boundaries and who would rather drink than be in your company. In my own recovery, I've found that real friends and family will want to help you protect and maintain a recovery-friendly environment.

In the early stages of my recovery, certain family members would taunt me by sticking a beer in my face and saying, "You know you miss this." One time, someone told me, "You're just weak." Unfortunately, some people are only satisfied if you're just as miserable as them. Those people don't want to see you succeed in your recovery. Let me set the record straight: sober people are far from weak. We are some of the strongest people I know, because we face life's challenges without relying on a sedative to cope. Sobriety empowers us with a clear and resilient mind, so we can fully embrace the purpose of our life's, rather than run away from it.

I don't want you to get discouraged; this is just what I have learned from my own recovery journey. Understand that loved ones may have opinions about your new life, but not everyone grasps or understands the depth of your experience. Be prepared for backlash and criticism, but consider this: Where were they when you were curled up alone in pain? Where were they during your destructive acts that shattered your family and home? Where were they when you got arrested, nearly died, or almost took someone else's life unknowingly? Where were they when you were screaming inside for help?

This is why you must be okay with people rejecting you in your pursuit of Sobriety.

"You've changed," someone once told me. And this was music to my ears, because I had. However, my change did not stick to their standards, but rather my own—in alignment with my newfound faith and life in recovery. While having a strong support system is important, I acknowledge that genuinely supportive friends and even family members can be quite difficult to come by. Therefore, I have immense gratitude for the support system I had around me, my beautiful wife and children. In 2010, when I was sobering up, my wife made a powerful commitment: "If you don't drink, I don't drink." These words resonated deeply within me, making my Sobriety so much easier because I knew we were in this together. Even though she was never a drinker like I was, my recovery became hers.

Perhaps the most challenging stage of the recovery process is this initial setting of boundaries, rules, and guidelines. Nonetheless, it is an essential step. There is nothing wrong with safeguarding your peace. It doesn't make you weak or cowardly; it actually makes you strong and wise, for you are setting yourself up for success.

The questions I typically get in response to this advice are: "So do I just never go out to eat where alcohol is? Do I just completely avoid family gatherings? Am I supposed to skip every sporting event or work-related Christmas party?"

You have to be brutally honest with yourself about where you are in your recovery. In regards to these questions, for me, it was yes. I steered clear of all areas and functions that had alcohol for many months, because I knew I wasn't strong enough then. But I started to make small appearances once my foundation was sturdier—once I was sure, deep down, I was going to be okay and not tempted by the presence of other drinkers.

If you are going to be around alcohol, you must secure that foundation first. Now that I'm 13 years into this, it doesn't bother me one bit. I can take my son to a boxing match and be unfazed, even though everyone in the venue is drinking. Yet, I remain mindful of my surroundings. Just because I feel safe and secure, doesn't mean I actively insert myself into situations with alcohol regularly. I deliberately choose when and where to navigate such environments.

Hear me out: You have to protect your surroundings, and discipline is required to do it.

2. You must be disciplined in your **priorities.**

Start each morning by asking yourself, "What are my priorities today? Do I have a clear direction and plan?" Personally, I find it helpful to make a weekly schedule, sometimes even monthly if the plans extend that far. My family is well aware of my schedule and priorities. They could easily tell you about my regular gym sessions, my

Monday class, which speaking engagements I have coming up, and when I am in and out of the office.

Over the years, I have developed a routine that centers around my priorities, which ensures that I stay focused. I have a checklist for the church, my personal life, and my home. One of my mentors emphasizes the importance of defining a daily win upon waking up—a reasonably-sized win that shows progress, change, and a step closer to your set goals. It's all about aiming to hit. This approach is the key to staying sober in life—waking up each day with a clear understanding of where you're headed and aligning your actions accordingly with your Sobriety.

What are your top priorities in life?

Certainly, unexpected things will arise. But remember, it's aiming to hit, not miss. My favorite piece of advice is the idea that what you write down is what you own. If you don't write it down, you don't own it, it's just a thought. Without putting thoughts into writing, they remain vanishing ideas. But when you write it down, it becomes a part of you. This principle is especially powerful in the recovery journey, transforming tasks into tangible commitments that sharpen your focus and add a level of ownership.

When you establish discipline in your surroundings and priorities, you'll be sailing down sober street for years to come. Without discipline, you're much more subject to falling back into drinking. Although it may not happen overnight, my goal is to prevent that outcome for you. I encourage you not to get comfortable or idle. Keep that pedal of discipline engaged so you can stay on the path of progress. As you read through this chapter, you're probably already considering areas in your surroundings and daily life that need improvement. Begin to examine your priorities as well. What do you want to accomplish today? What about this month? You've got this, friend; keep going! Let's get unstuck together.

Chapter 5

Generational Patterns

"You're breaking generational patterns. That's why things don't come so easy for you. You're the one your bloodline has been waiting for."
- Thomas Mofolo

When I started writing my first book, I shared a few chapters with my mom. However, when she finished reading, I didn't get the reaction I expected. With sadness in her eyes, she uttered, "I didn't know that's how you felt, and I'm sorry if I caused that."

I was shocked, of course.

The purpose of letting her read my book was not to evoke feelings of guilt or sorrow; rather, it was an effort to show her that I was evolving into someone she could feel proud of—an author and, hopefully, a helping hand to those in need. The chapters she read were simply a glimpse into my heart growing up. I believe that a man's heart is a deep cavern of emotions that we typically try to cover up and hide. As men, we're taught not to cry or openly express our feelings, so if or when they do arise, it often comes as a shock.

Though, I do think those chapters made her realize that there were some things she could have changed if she wanted to. Perhaps it reminded her of some personal experiences she tried to forget, revealing thoughts and emotions I had never shared with her. For instance, I had kept silent about the emotional toll her divorce took on me, the deep-rooted grief I felt when my grandparents died in a car accident caused by a drunk driver, the discomfort I experienced when we moved to a different state, and the impact her aggressive shouting matches with my father had on my tender heart. I carried so much anger, hurt, and insecurity growing up. And she was never aware of these bottled-up emotions or my troubled thought processes as a child and teenager, because I never told her. Now let me say this, my mother is a remarkable person. She was a hardworking single mom who did everything she could to see that my brother and I had what we needed to survive, even if she lacked. She shielded me when I needed support, and, to this day, she will never fully grasp the extent of her influence on my life.

Now, I certainly cannot claim that the family I'm currently raising is perfect—far from it! I'm well aware that my family and I are both a work in progress. Nevertheless, my aim is to inspire families to break free from repeating the same mistakes their parents made and their parents' parents made before them. Generational patterns are real, and they can be challenging to overcome—a reality I witnessed firsthand with my own family during my drinking years. I can't tell you how many birthday parties, celebrations, and sporting events I attended, where I was either intoxicated, passed out, or had somehow made a fool of myself. But in the Hispanic culture, we just write it off as normal because it's what we observed growing up. I mean, how could we throw a birthday party for our kids and not find a way to make it about ourselves? I've noticed that we will make any excuse just to drink, even if it means overtaking a ten-year-old's special day.

I can confess with absolute confidence that I've made my share of mistakes as a father that I wish I could undo.

Even today, I'm not immune to messing up, as it's an inherent part of the process of living and learning. However, I want to emphasize this change: I no longer desire to drink, and I refuse to make the same mistakes that brought so much pain upon my family back then. While I don't claim perfection, I've definitely transformed for the better.

Acknowledging how widespread generational patterns are today, it's become quite uncommon to find families still intact. The divorce rate in America is high, forcing numerous kids into a situation where they must bounce around from house to house on the weekends. As parents engage in ugly custody battles, too many kids bear witness to the tangible harm and emotional distress caused by divorce. As parents, we tend to think our kids don't see or know, but my experience proves otherwise. Kids are like sponges, hearing and feeling everything their parents go through. And their emotional pain is more intense during custody battles; we just fail to notice.

Though, the growing percentage of kids growing up without both parents present is not solely a consequence of divorce; it's also due to parents being locked up, in rehab, or stuck on the streets with drug or alcohol addictions. These situations occur much more frequently than we care to acknowledge—a reality I'm directly familiar with through my involvement in a mentorship program for the city. In these sessions, I engage with countless kids, listening to their stories of suffering and witnessing the pain and sorrow they endure due to family dysfunction rooted in generational patterns. Somehow, alcohol abuse seems to be a common factor.

Consider how much brokenness is transferred from one generation to the next and how much rebuilding must take place to heal. In America today, we find ourselves wrestling with an Alcoholism crisis—a vicious cycle that's not only passed down within families, but also encouraged within a society that tends to overlook the source of pain and resort to self-medication as a temporary escape.

I must admit, I'm grateful that I grew up in the 90s, when society's pressures were already challenging enough. Now, with social media, I can't even imagine the additional burdens our kids deal with, leading them to turn to many coping mechanisms like cutting, having sex, drinking, using drugs, or, even more tragically, attempting suicide. Reflecting on this, how many of you can say you started drinking alcohol at a young age? If so, why? What were you dealing with? What was swirling around in your young heart and mind? Was it influenced by your environment, modeled by those you looked up to? Or did you turn to it as an escape, drawn to the way it made you feel?

What I do know is this: as a society, we've developed a pattern of coping with challenges in unhealthy ways—a trend that tends to start in our developing years. There is always an underlying cause for why we do what we do, and understanding this cause is crucial for breaking free from the destructive pattern.

Think about a powerful pattern in your life that has been holding you down for a long time.

Unknowingly repeating the mistakes of our parents and family, whether emotionally or physically, traps us in a generational stronghold. We find ourselves dealing with life and all its brokenness in the same unhealthy ways, often without realizing that it isn't normal. However, I am here to tell you that this cycle can be broken as I see it play out with my own children today. If I would of stayed the course of drinking, I would be picking up my kids off from the floors, in the bars drunk. It's a pattern that must stop.

It's usually much easier to see the pattern play out in others. How many times have you heard someone say, "I learned this from my mom" or "I have my dad's bad habits"? In others, it's quite obvious, but we tend to have a blind spot when it comes to awareness of our own behaviors, especially when it's an issue that demands an effort from us to change. That's the generational stronghold at work.

Why do we see this recurring pattern of generations cycling in and out of prison, from fathers to sons to grandsons? The same question applies to the revolving door of rehab. A stronghold serves one purpose: to maintain) a pattern. It consistently steers you towards destructive habits that cripple your potential and derail you from your purpose.

As I reflect on my life, it's clear that I was once caught in this exact situation, unknowingly repeating the same mistakes I had learned from my family.

Did I really need to have a beer in my hand at every family function, Sunday game, or BBQ I hosted? Was it necessary to turn every gathering at my house into party where my little girls watched me drink, scream, and act like an idiot, surrounded by intoxicated people when they should have been peacefully asleep? There was certainly no reason for me to send my middle daughter to fetch me a beer from the fridge, let alone give her a sip when she handed it to me. Nor did I have to degrade or belittle the mother of my kids simply because I was the man of the house and my word was law. Throughout my whole life, I had mistakenly believed that I needed to dominate conversations and arguments. Rarely did I cry or express how I felt—I was a very bitter, prideful, and angry man. Growing up, I was under the impression that the man had to be in total control or he was not a man at all. Little did I know, I was carrying out so many generational patterns on an emotional, physical, and relational level, simply because it was all I knew.

While we are certainly responsible for our own actions and should not cast blame onto any of our family (they are simply repeating the patterns that were passed down to them), it's essential to acknowledge that children will echo the voices of their parents. It makes me think of how my granddaughter will walk around the house saying, "hello," "bye," and "love you," because it's what we say to her. Unfortunately, this trend of mimicking what is seen and heard continues in older children and teenagers. As discussed in the Chapter 2, there is always a root cause. And, as parents, we must be willing to assume responsibility for the roots we instill in our children's hearts and minds.

Imagine the transformation in ourselves and our kids if one day we could learn and break those generational patterns. Visualize a reality where we are secure in our identities, free from insecurities, and openly expressive of our emotions. Imagine feeling unconditionally loved instead of isolated and rejected, being faithful to our spouses till death do us part, breaking free from depression and anxiety and being filled with REAL happiness. Picture putting an end to poverty in our families, choosing to stay out of rehabs and prisons, and learning how to heal our lives rather than take them. Imagine breaking the chains of Alcoholism. What would this look like for our families?

Yet we continue to recreate the mistakes of our ancestors. The questions remains: when will we learn? When will we muster up the courage and strength to declare, "Right here, right now, it stops with me"? "It stops with my daughter, with my son, and with my grandkids." Someone needs to step up, and if you're reading this, it might as well be you.

I love my blood family deeply, yet the legacy passed down by my great-great Grandpa and Grandma has presented many challenges we still struggle with today—challenges I'm sure they inherited from their parents and so on. Both of my great-great grandparents died due to Alcoholism. Grandpa was shot in a bar, and Grandma drank herself to death. Since then, their influence has continued to descend through the family with force.

The purpose of this chapter is to prompt a close examination of your life. I urge you to honestly ask yourself, "Am I repeating these generational patterns? Have these generational patterns led to issues in my life and my family's lives?" If the answer is yes to either of these, it's essential to understand that these patterns can be broken, and how they can be broken is what the rest of this book will cover. By the time you finish reading, you will have developed healthy habits to break those strongholds, as well as a positive attitude to outweigh depression and defeat. Stay focused, stay committed, and stay encouraged!

I firmly believe you can do this, no matter what your past or recent experiences look like—no matter how deep-rooted those generational patterns may seem, and no matter how dreadful you perceive the challenges to be.

Today, I am the first author, the first pastor, and the first person in my family to travel and speak throughout the United States, seeing places I'd never thought or dreamed of seeing. I've written a script, produced, and assembled a short film about my life, with hopes that it may one day become a full-fledged movie. I am the first to have a documentary made about my life, and the first to be featured in magazines, news broadcasts, and organizational interviews, all centered around my transformation. I share these accomplishments not to boast about myself, but to highlight that no one is too far gone to be reached. No one is too entangled in unhealthy generational patterns to make a positive turnaround for themselves and their family.

I always teach my kids and others to dream big, recognizing that dreaming often involves breaking free from life's norms. Generational patterns prevent us from really living and dreaming. And continuously playing out these unhealthy family patterns makes it difficult to build a fulfilling life. So let's work on breaking those patterns and dreaming big for our families. I certainly am and want to see you do the same.

Chapter 6

Hi, my name is "Muddy Situation"

"You could always go buy another box, but broken crayons still color."
-David Weaver

Alcoholism isn't just life-shattering; it's soul-sucking. When you find yourself gazing up from a pit you've created, beat down and dirty, know that you can always wipe the filth from your eyes and start anew. The slightest glimmer of light can lead you out of the darkest of holes, enabling you to dust yourself off, pick up the pieces, and grant yourself a second chance—a new hope for tomorrow.

I sincerely believe that's what every person desires when confronted with the depths of Alcoholism. For some, hitting rock bottom is an unbearable burden, a weight that reshapes what was once familiar in our lives—our careers, families, and futures—into something unknown. This struggle leaves behind a trail of raw, unfelt emotions, which we will explore in this chapter.

After years of continuous drinking, I found myself in a similar situation. Sasha (the mother of my kids) reached her breaking point nine years into our relationship when she decided to leave me, taking the kids with her. The sudden shift from being a full-time dad to now being separated from my kids was crushing. It also meant going from waking up in my own bed to now sleeping on my friends' couches, bouncing around from house to house in search of a place to lay my head.

One muggy afternoon, as I walked to the local store, I found myself wrestling with my thoughts. With every step, I battled; with every upward glance towards the sky, I sighed. Rehab had proved ineffective for me, as I couldn't bear the environment. It forced me to hold a magnifying glass up to my life, revealing every ugly detail and every secret chamber I wished to conceal. My Alcoholism was hopelessly exposed and I didn't like it, no matter how hard I tried to pretend I was okay. Now that everything was in the open, I could see clearly what I had become. I wondered how I'd gotten so lost, deceiving myself into believing I had control over my drinking, only to realize I didn't. Now that I was out of rehab, aimlessly wandering the streets of El Paso, I found myself back at the bar later that night.

These kind of scenarios appear in movies all the time, but you never expect to experience them yourself. Many songs portray images like walking alone in the rain, but living them is an entirely different feeling. Those raw emotions you feel right now have one purpose: to be a spark for learning and growth. Let them drive you, rather than swallow you whole! You know how it goes in wrestling—someone must win.

I want to touch on three aspects of a "Muddy Situation." Picture yourself deep in the pit, flinging mud down from your clothes and preparing yourself for the climb. Before you do, I urge you to learn how to deal with these three things, because if you don't, climbing out of that hole will be a much greater challenge.

Number 1 is **Embarrassment**.

Listen very carefully: you have nothing to be embarrassed about. Everyone needs help at some point in life. I struggled with embarrassment and fear of judgement for so long—worrying about what others would say or how they'd treat me. That shame and embarrassment only prolonged my drinking and acknowledgement of needing help. In my family, no one ever went to rehab or even talked about their problems. I came from that prideful, macho, Hispanic family line, where the solution to every problem was to simply push through. Expressing our emotions wasn't part of my upbringing, so I just learned to bottle up mine, keeping my weaknesses and struggles hidden from everyone.

In my eyes, getting help was a sign of weakness, so I kept quiet. But you should never be embarrassed about seeking help or considering a treatment center to break the cycle of addiction. Never be ashamed of wanting to live a better and healthier life. People can be quick to judge what they don't understand, but that's no reason to walk your sober journey with embarrassment. Embrace all the help, all the faith, and all the programs and tools you need to stay sober.

Number 2 is **Guilt**.

If we are not careful, this will eat at us like acid. The more guilt we allow in, the more corrosive that acid becomes. I know what you're saying: "You have no idea what kind of damage I have caused in my family," or "It's so messed up right now, I don't know if I can ever get out of this."

I get it! You hurt a lot of people, broke a lot of promises, and shattered a lot of dreams. However, you cannot hang on to that guilt forever. If you do, it'll trap you in circles, dragging you down again and again and preventing your growth in recovery. You have to accept that what's done is done and let go of the past if you want to move forward. Apologize and make amends with as many people as possible, then set your sights on Sobriety. Things will certainly arise that'll trigger your guilt; just don't allow yourself to dwell on them for too long.

I remember when I was in Texas and my family gave me a second chance, returning home so we could began repairing our lives together. It was a season of building from the ground up. I was working for a pest control company, and we were staying with my in-laws until we could afford our own place. On one occasion, I recall going to this lovely home to treat. I stepped into the kids' bedrooms to spray the baseboards—one room was princess-themed and the other was sports—when suddenly, all of that guilt came rushing back, eating up my insides as if I had swallowed a bucket of acid.

At that moment, it struck me—my kids once had their own rooms and a place to call home. Now, they were sharing a room at my in-laws', all because my drinking had destroyed that for them. Alcoholism truly shakes the foundations of families' lives.

However, I quickly snapped out of it! With a positive outlook, I affirmed, "We may not have a place to call home right now, but one day, we will!" Whenever guilt creeps into your heart and mind, just remind yourself with that simple statement: "One day, things will turn around for the better."

One day, you will finish school; one day, you will have a job; and, one day, you will get to share your struggles and make it up to your family. One day, you'll recover everything you've lost, and, one day, everything that has torn you down will make you stronger. Personally, this "one-day" mentality is what got me through tough times of guilt. So get this in your heart: whatever you've lost or left undone due to alcohol, whatever you've sacrificed to support your addictive habits, and whatever dreams seemed shattered—you will reclaim and accomplish it all. One day!

Number 3 is **Regret**.

There is a rule in life: you cannot see what's in front of you if you're always looking behind. This principle holds true in the recovery process as well. You will never get out of your muddy situation if your gaze remains fixed on the ground; you must lift your head high and focus on the light if you want to make strides in your recovery. There may be times when you have to claw and scratch your way out, but the reward will definitely justify the struggle.

I can't count how many times those "what-if's" and "should-have's" plagued my mind. Questions like, "What if I had gotten help sooner?" or, "I should have just listened from the start." We tend to believe these reflections will somehow make us feel better, when in reality, it's the opposite. While looking back can help prevent us from repeating the same mistakes, we can never go back and erase the past. Therefore, some things are simply better left unspoken and undisturbed, allowing time and space for healing.

We must learn to forgive ourselves to release that regret, and enjoy the present moment while focusing on the future. There are so many blessings and opportunities before you—the promise of a sober future, a life dedicated to assembling the pieces and arranging them in their rightful places.

Understand this: It's impossible to enjoy a better tomorrow if constantly focused on a troubled yesterday.

You'd be surprised how many people remain stuck in the past. It's easy to do, because it's what we're familiar with, as the unknown often makes us uneasy. Yet the true beauty of life unfolds when we can reflect on the completed masterpiece of our experiences, knowing that our pain and suffering have shaped us into who we are today. Life's challenges should always be used to our advantage. Our pain is never wasted because it reveals our greatest strengths. No matter how muddy your current situation, remember that the only person who owes you a better life and future is you. I've seen too many people walk out of jail, prison, or rehab and act like the world owes them something. And that false expectation will keep them in the mud much longer. A beautiful life isn't owed to you, but you owe it to yourself to create one!

Remember, embarrassment, guilt and regret will only keep you buried in the mud. So clean yourself up, fix your gaze high, and let's climb out of this hole one step at a time. I know things look dark and dreary now, but the light is only one choice away.

Just know that people stay dirty because they choose to, and people get clean because they need to.

I needed to get better for myself and my family, and the same holds true for you! It's a muddy situation, but that mud is filled with possibilities for new life and growth. Stay encouraged.

Chapter 7

Hi, my name Is "Alcoholism"

"As an Alcoholic, you will violate your standards quicker than you can lower them."
-Robin Williams

Hello, my name is Alcoholism. I've been around for a very long time, and I'm still a main source of entertainment today. I'm kind of a big deal. You can find me everywhere: on hats, t-shirts, billboards, and every social media platform you can think of. I even have my own aisle at the grocery store. I'm also found at birthday parties, company celebrations, and BBQ's. Depending on your church, you can even find me at Bible studies—that's right! One time I was invited to a Bible group. They drank and prayed, but little did those people know, someone in that group was two months sober. One drink from me sent her on a three-month binge. I don't think I belong in Bible studies, but that's just me. I'm probably the most expensive thing around and here's why: I come with a price, but not everyone just pays with money; some pay with their lives, dreams, and even their families. I can't count how many goals I've destroyed and families I've broken due to generational patterns. I have gotten so many people fired, ruined so many careers, and caused so many people to drop out of school and even life. I'm the reason divorce rates are so high in America.

I start off as social. I start off as fun. People consume me to ease the stress. They drink to unwind, chill, take a load off, and sometimes just forget. Poor people!

Their lives seem to be very rough; they flock to the bars to consume me. They lie to get to me, fight to get to me, and give their last dollar for me. Many start small, but disconnect from their hearts and minds, quickly losing control. They black out and ask, "Do you remember what happened last night?" I wonder how many have woken up next to a stranger naked—how many kids have been birthed because of me. That's what I do. I make people forget. I disrupt and derail their lives, draining every bit of energy they have left. This is the world people want to live in, so this is the world I provide. I make them forget their lives, so they can momentarily live in me.

Hello, my name is Alcoholism. I make people numb. I'm not just a social activity; I'm a cover-up for the hurt, struggle, and pain people harbor from childhood. They don't want to feel, so I make them care and feel less. For that worry-free moment, I am theirs, and they are mine. I wrap my arms around them with false security, peace, and strength. Their thoughts, spirit, heart, and life, in the moment, are mine! Many turn to me with burdens so heavy, I can feel it. Some have been abused emotionally and sexually. Some grew up in rough households without parents. Some feel abandoned. Some struggle with depression. I wish I could tell them I won't make those dark thoughts any lighter. All I do is unleash them like a raging tidal wave, crashing through every rock and branch until I have them surrounded. They may try to kick and come up for air, but eventually they'll drown—in those thoughts and in me. I'll be the first to tell you I do not bring healing; I bring false closure. When our moment together has passed, you'll still wake up to your life in the morning. Those thoughts, hurts, and burdens will never go away with me.

But no matter how bad it hurts, how much it destroys them, or how unbearable their lives seem, they keep coming back. I am their security blanket.

Hello, my name is Alcoholism. I steer so many kids down the same road as their parents—as I did with their parents and their parents' parents. Remember, I have been around for a very long time. I open doors for kids they wish they never knocked on, even if the parents do their best to keep them locked. Though, sometimes the parents are the ones to leave the doors open. They forget they hold the key, so the kids just walk right through. While some may claim that their kids' relationship with me has nothing to do with them, if I could speak to these parents, I'd say, "Kids are products of their environment." And that's the hard truth.

Hello, my name is Alcoholism. I create numerous health problems. I can take a perfectly good liver and turn it inside out. I've taken many young people to their graves with DWI's and sent many more to prison. People do some weird stuff when they're under my control. It's like they don't think or understand what they are doing. All they do is act and suffer the consequences later.

Hello, my name is Alcoholism. I see you in the club, on the dance floor, at your friend's house, around the table. I see you with every smile, laugh, smirk, shout, and tear. Your friends and family see one version, but I see the real you. When the fun wears off, music stops, and drinks stop flowing, I see you crying in the corner of your shower, lying on the floor retching. I see you when your soul screams "HELP," your tears say "tired," and your vomit cries "afraid." I see you when you're angry at home, throwing things, breaking stuff. I see you when you bleed, when you cut, when you yell, "I can't no more!" yet your body echoes "more." You suffer in silence, and nobody knows but me. I'd like to tell you you're safe with me. But you're not.

I see your tired kids and family, wondering which person they'll get this week or weekend. If I could speak to you, I'd say, "Get help now." You can only do this for so long before you break—before your body shuts down and cries, "No more!" I know you think I can take your pain away—take everything away!—but I can't. Don't keep feeding me and hurting you. Don't keep allowing me to entertain you. I know you're seeking and trying to fill that void.

But it's at the end of the bottle, at the end of the "last call," that you will still be empty.

Sincerely,

Alcoholism

Chapter

8

Destroy the Image,
Break the Cycle.

"What are you willing to give up, in order to become who you really need to be?"

-Elizabeth Gilbert

Why do we want to drink? Why do we love to torture ourselves with morning sickness? You know we have a problem culturally when people who wake up with a throbbing headache and feel like death, will declare, "I am never drinking again," then have a bottle in their hands four days later. Most likely, we saw this growing up. Maybe we grew up thinking that the only way to have fun in life was to drink at every function and outing. Maybe it's just what people do, right? Instead of going out to eat, opening birthday cards, and celebrating their twenty-first birthdays in peace, people go to happy hour and get drunk legally rather than undercover—or was that just me? When this day comes, there's no more hiding, and a new generation of drinkers are born.

The beast of Alcoholism no longer must be tamed—it's out in public, destroying whatever gets in its way.

I will never forget when my mom opened up about her family's battle with Alcoholism. I grew up witnessing my mom struggle with her own share of alcohol, as well as my dad and the rest of my family. To this day, some of them still struggle. I remember the day I vowed to never turn out like that, believing I was stronger. But in the end, I was worse, and found myself entangled in the stronghold of my family's Alcoholism.

I also strongly recall a newspaper clipping about my Grandma and Grandpa being killed by a drunk driver in 1985. Alcoholism killed them and the driver, and now it was on track to kill their grandson (me). Everything alcohol touches, eventually it will destroy. If you don't get a handle on it, you will be next.

That doesn't mean we should cast blame on our parents or their parents—they were caught in the cycle passed down from generations before them. It's just that no one really questioned it. If a marriage failed or someone got locked up due to alcohol, no one said anything. That was just life. Drinking Alcohol was just made to seem normal growing up. When someone died from Alcoholism, no one found it odd that the same drink that killed them was the drink we use to celebrate their life with after the funeral. It's that pattern that we have been talking about in this book. And that pattern will continue in our families, unless someone wakes up and starts asking questions. And makes those changes that are needed.

Having that attitude of "it's just the way it is" is a prison sentence mentally for ourselves and our families. But people have to see and experience the destruction of Alcoholism firsthand to fully grasp this. How many sons and daughters would be spared, how many dreams would be fulfilled, if only they could see and understand Alcoholism for what is truly is?

Here's what I mean by **"Destroy the image, Break the cycle"**:

Do you remember in "Enter the Dragon" when Bruce Lee sees his and his enemy's image everywhere he turns?

Many times, I hear people say, "I need to start fresh and move somewhere new to recover," which I understand. However, just like in the movie, no matter where you go, your enemy's image will be there in the mirror, staring you in the face and tempting you with its tricks. No matter which way you turn, the enemy is laughing at you waiting for you to fall.

So if you really want to break this cycle, you must destroy the image, otherwise it will follow you to the grave. It waits for you!—like a lion stalking its prey. It lurks, it sits, it watches. You can't see it because the grass is tall. But just when you're at your lowest, weakest, and most vulnerable, it attacks. Without warning, its jaws wrapped around your neck, you can't breathe or even move. You're wounded, dying inside with every shallow breath. You sit there in pain and defeat. The enemy has won. Now you are back to your own ways, with every drink, taking off days—maybe years—of your life.

Every drink strips us of who we are and who we are becoming. Every drink numbs us from the inside out, yet we don't even see it. But one day, when it's all said and done, we will! We will see the devastation Alcoholism has caused. Often, it's only when our lives begin to unravel that we notice. If we don't destroy this image—this belief that drinking is a part of our identity—it will kill us very slowly.

All it takes to break that cycle is for one person to decide, "I don't need alcohol"—"I don't need it to have a good time," and "I don't need to bring it around my family." With one choice, you could be the one to break that cycle for your kids and grandkids—and for who knows how many generations to come. While every individual has a choice, your influence is everything.

Some may dismiss this chapter because they don't want to face the truth. We do what we want and live how we want, and nobody can tell us otherwise, even if we know we are wrong—even if we know it will cost us something. It has and will continue to destroy many families and marriages, steering many down the wrong path, with some even ending in suicide. The reality is that Alcoholism doesn't just hurt the person who drinks; that hurt oozes out to everyone else, trapping families in a cycle they never asked to be in. We get to a point where we don't even know what to say anymore.

My hope is that, as you continue to read this book, you will analyze yourself and your family line—not out of criticism or judgement, but to recognize that some things must change. And it starts with you and I. Walking around the house with a beer in my hand and having late-night parties followed by hungover mornings doesn't put my family in a position to win. You need to view your situation as bigger than you. Now that my granddaughter is living with us, the environment I create is even more important. And it brings me joy that my granddaughter doesn't have to see her grandpa hungover like my kids did. She doesn't have to see me falling apart and slowly dying inside like my kids did. What she does see is Grandpa reading his Bible and drinking his coffee. What she hears is Grandpa praying for his family, which she joins some mornings, sitting on my lap in prayer.

When I leave this world, I want to at least know that I tried to set my family up for success—that I did my best to set a positive example for them. It would kill me inside to know that my kids or grandkids died of Alcoholism as a result of my example, with seeds that I planted in their lives when they were younger. Because when seeds get planted, they get watered and grow. So we must plant good seeds for our family—seeds of Sobriety, success, purpose, and living.

But we must destroy that negative image to sow positive seeds. And here is why that can be difficult: **Selfishness** and **Pride** have blinded our need for change.

Selfishness says, "This is my life, and I can do what I want. I am grown even if I know my actions will hurt others."

Pride says, "Who are you or anyone to tell me how to live my life?"

We must learn how to tame those prideful and selfish voices—the ones that make excuses for our actions, habits, and words—because, once again, we are the KEY to breaking the cycle of Alcoholism, not just for ourselves but for the family we'll never meet.

I learned to drink because I saw it—at every birthday party, celebration, and family function. If the people I looked up to and respected drank, it must have been okay for me too. Family members would give me sips of alcohol at the age of 14, unaware that seeds were not only planted, they were already sprouting. When stress would overshadow my family, they drank, unaware that their stress-reliever would soon become mine.

If you take anything away from this chapter, let it be this: Every individual has the power to choose. However, when bad habits form due to years in the making, breaking those habits can feel like a death. But the other side of that death is a light brighter than you could imagine—a light that can illuminate the lives of everyone around you. It all starts with you, friend. The image of your past self, with all your past habits, must die.

"Destroy the Image, Break the Cycle."

Chapter 9

Hi, my name Is "Sober"

Hi, my name is Sober. Life is not boring. You wake up with no more regrets—no more headaches or sickness. There is something wonderful about not looking over your shoulder anymore. It's over this side of the fence that you want to be and stay. Challenges will come up. And they may seem difficult to face now that you don't have the bottle, especially since your feelings have been drowned out for so long. But you must gather the strength to stay on my side of the fence—the strength to process and feel through every challenge life throws your way.

Hi, my name is Sober. You will lose friends over the months. Because, let's be honest, they don't know why you're not showing up to gatherings anymore and drinking with them. While some may not say it, they think you're pretty lame and boring now. Don't be surprised if they don't speak to you for a while. If you want to hang out with me, you will have to let go of them.

Everyone will have an opinion, but it's likely none of them will be helpful. Most will want to tear you down, and few, if any, will want to build you up. If this is your case, you've got some shifting to do in your social circle. If you do have a support system in your pursuit of me, welcome it! You'll need all the help you can get. Good friends are hard to find in your recovery, so if you have them, keep them!

Hi, my name is Sober. Let's get you dried up. Your stomach will twist and your body will hurt, as you've been on this path for so long. Don't expect to walk away without a few black eyes. Don't think alcohol will let you go without a fight, but it's a fight that you must face, knowing that no one else can do it for you. You must get up and keep swinging your way towards me. Though, it will require complete trust in the process. Sleepless nights, headaches, mood swings—let it all come. If you want to walk with me, you'll have to stand up and fight every day of your life, but it will all be worth it. I know what you're thinking: "Can I really do this? Can I really stop drinking?" Hi, my name is Sober, and yes, you can.

Hi, my name is Sober. You have come too far to go back. You're doing great! You're going to your classes; you're going to therapy. Wait… Where are you going? Why are you thinking about drinking again? So you had a bad day? I get it. It's getting hard. But you've come such a long way. Don't you see all the progress you've already accomplished? Ride this wave out and wait till tomorrow. Don't drink based one bad emotional day; we all have them. Tomorrow's blessings are coming. Can I be honest with you? I am afraid for you. I've watched you drink your way so deep into Alcoholism. You have a bad heart, bad liver, and overall bad health. If you turn your back on me now, this could be it for you—that drink could kill you. So you must not give up. Redemption is possible. If you can stay sober with me for a day, you can stay sober for life.

Hi, my name is Sober. I am a new way of thinking and living. You will probably have emotions come up that you've never felt before. Don't panic! It's normal. For years, you have learned to suppress and avoid these emotions. You think life was tough with Alcoholism? How about now with me? I may be tough to be around, but I'll show you that you're built differently. I'll make you see that you're stronger than you think and, if you're up for it, what you're really made of.

Hi, my name is Sober. Don't expect your spouse to be excited just yet because you stopped drinking. This will take some time with your kids as well. Remember, you are doing this for you first. I know you want them to be happy for you, but let's be honest. How many times did you say "this will be my last drink"? Don't get discouraged; give them time. Just stay the course and be consistent, and you'll see them start to come around. They love you and want the best for you. Please believe it and stay motivated.

Hi, my name is Sober. Before I go, I want you to know I am so proud of you. Not many people get to where you are now. They give up too soon, allowing that scorpion tail to strike, stinging them with relapse and discouragement. It pumps their veins with the poison of failure and doubt, clouding their vision and keeping them stuck.

But look where you are now—on my side of the fence. Who would have thought? I did! I was just waiting for you to get tired and stop fighting yourself—waiting for you to surrender. And I am beyond proud of you.

Get this in your heart before I say goodbye: a life with me is dedication, hard work, and self-discipline. It won't be handed to you. It's getting up every single day and putting in the work. But when you look in the mirror, you'll see a sober face instead of a tired one. You'll see a face that looks free instead of a face that looks enslaved—the lively face we all have been waiting to see. Take care of yourself. You're doing it.

Hi, my name is Sober, and I want the best for you.

Sincerely,

Sober

Chapter 10

Hi, my name Is "Forgiveness"

"Forgiveness is not weak. It takes courage to face and overcome powerful emotions."
-Desmond Tutu

When I travel to prisons and rehabs and speak to men and women in recovery, I always ask these two questions:

"Have you forgiven yourself?"

"Have you forgiven others?"

You'd be surprised how many look down at the floor in response. It's a look I am familiar with—a look of defeat. It's when our inner being utters, "I don't think I can," or "What does that even look like?" Though, I believe it runs even deeper.

Forgiveness comes in all shapes and sizes, and the lack of it damages the heart more than we realize. It affects how we act, react, and live our lives. I wonder how many people operate in bitterness and resentment daily. We say we are okay, yet deep down, we hurt—a hurt that has been stacked on our hearts for years. For this reason, the key to getting sober is to forgive ourselves and others. Many people I believe are walking in recovery still hurt and wounded.

We think about our lives and all the "what ifs" and "should haves", constantly casting blame on others and ourselves. We keep dwelling on a past that can never be changed, rather than a future we can strive to improve. Staying stuck in our hurt with grudges and grief will only keep us in a state of dependency—dependency on an identity based in the past to inform how we should think and live today, and dependency on alcohol to drown out our unprocessed emotions when they return with greater force each time.

I want you to think about this for a minute:

Hurt will always drive us to something.

"What is it driving you to?"

"What does this have to do with getting Sober?" you might ask. "With breaking those generational strongholds in our families?"

I don't know about you, but I have people in my family that still hold grudges with other family members today. They still think and talk about it, are still angry and bitter, even though these events happened many years ago. I have even seen some refuse to talk to each other for years. When we see this as children, we grow up thinking it's okay not to forgive others. Then we carry on with that same unforgiving heart and hold grudges like our parents and their parents did.

While I never want to dismiss anyone's hurt—it's a valid emotion that everyone experiences—how long should we hold on to it? How long should we allow that hurt to fester in our hearts and minds? Once it drives us to the point of drinking or other unhealthy habits, it's certainly gone too far. I think many people see forgiveness as a kind of competition. They hold out, thinking the other person will apologize or take accountability first, so they don't have to. However, next thing you know, it's been years of misery, living in past pains with an unsettled heart.

So it's up to you to break that cycle of unforgiveness, but here's the secret: before you can forgive others, you must forgive yourself. This is why many people find it impossible to release grudges on others—they're still holding grudges against themselves.

This state of unforgiveness is a slow and silent misery if not dealt with in a healthy way. Hurt stacks on hurt, and that weight becomes unbearable. Eventually, our knees will buckle if we don't do something.

In theory, forgiveness is simple, though it's a choice you must make daily. It's not about forgetting, but about allowing your heart and mind to heal. It's about choosing not to let a simple emotion control your life.

You have to let go of the past, because the past won't let go of you. If you don't, it will continue to rob you of your present, draining your energy and keeping you stuck seeking out ways to fill that void.

Before discussing how to forgive yourself, I want to address how you can forgive others. Because while we have certainly let people down due to our Alcoholism, others have hurt us as well.

Whether you are disappointed in one or both parents for being absent in your youth, or upset with a spouse for hurting you with their words or actions, forgiveness is up to you. It's a one way street, not a four way stop.

If you're spiritual, surrender that hurt to God and let him handle it. He will give you the strength to forgive. Remember, forgiveness is not letting people off the hook; it's choosing to break the cycle of silence and tension so you can heal.

If you're not spiritual, every day you must wake up and simply choose not to be bitter or angry.

Let's learn to heal each other with forgiveness instead of damage each other with grudges. Grudges harden the heart, turning it into stone. And once that heart is hardened, we feel justified in our right to be mad, hurt, and resentful for a very long time. It's much easier to forgive and move on than it is to dig our heels in and let our hearts get to that point.

When I was in recovery, I was so angry and bitter at Sasha, now my wife. We were separated during the beginning of my recovery days, and I was angry at her for leaving me. I was upset because she said she would always be there for me, and when I needed her the most, she turned her back on me. When I needed her smile, warmth, words of encouragement, and love, she was not there. When I would talk to her about the kids, just hearing her voice would make me so upset. I had formed an attitude of bitterness and blame.

Though, my grudge wasn't hurting her; it was only hurting myself. She was my best friend for so long and my Alcoholism had pushed her away. My Alcoholism made her second in my life and tore her down as a woman and human being. I had to really look deep into why I wasn't forgiving her. I kept trying to justify why I wasn't, but they were all simply excuses. Because when you point out other's faults, it's easy to overlook your own. I knew I needed to begin my own healing journey before I could genuinely forgive.

And no matter how wronged I felt or how justified I wanted to be, I had to forgive. Learning to forgive myself allowed me to forgive Sasha, which in turn allowed me to heal more. And I believe it allowed her to heal as well. There truly is so much power in forgiveness. All we have to do is make that choice.

Once again, there is an order when it comes to forgiveness. Before you can forgive others, you must forgive yourself.

But forgiving yourself is much easier said than done, so I want to leave you with two things to think about as you work towards forgiveness in your journcy of Sobriety.

1. Forgiveness is the greatest gift you can give yourself.

Again, if you're spiritual, you know God has already forgiven you. He forgives all your wrongdoings, mess-ups, and mistakes. So why not forgive yourself?

It's difficult to forgive yourself when all you do is dwell on the past. Whatever the case may be for you, that past is like a black cloud that keeps rolling overhead if you let it. And there will be people that trigger you by bringing up old things and reminding you of past pains.

People will always bring up the old you when they refuse to get to know the new you.

Here is what helped me learn to forgive myself: I had to admit that I was truly an alcoholic, and one hundred percent of the pain and hurt I was experiencing was due to my addiction. Now that I was in my right mind, I needed to let go of all the damage that was done when I was not in my right mind. I didn't want to have a pity party anymore. I wanted to move forward and experience the true freedom that forgiving myself would bring. And I now had the clarity and capacity to do so. Though, it was a daily walk towards that gift. It's something you must get up every day and affirm, "Today I forgive myself." You must look in the mirror and know you are a new person. Don't look at yourself and see a failure; see a future. See forgiveness and purpose. See a person that made it. And before you know it, that black cloud will roll out and the sun will begin to shine.

How many of you lived in one house growing up? I certainly didn't. I had several houses as a child and even as an adult, each with its good and bad seasons. Now that I don't live there anymore, I can drive by any of them and recall events with detachment. And this is how you must approach your past: "I don't live there anymore." View each memory as a season of learning or unlearning. What's done is done—you no longer live there—so it's time to forgive yourself. Take a moment to close your eyes and say "I forgive myself for ________." And practice this every day.

Forgiving yourself requires a lot of these daily pep talks and positive thoughts. Consider this for a moment: you can never travel back to the year 1995 or 2000 or whichever years you spent drinking your life away. You can't go back and change what you said, did, or should have done. What you can change, however, is what you say and do today to steer your life in whichever direction you want. If you keep clinging to that old house—that old version of yourself with all its painful memories—it will kill you mentally, spiritually, and physically. Keep looking forward so you can begin to heal and invest in the house you really want. You owe that to yourself. Remember, you don't live there anymore!

2. Process your anger.

I can recall so many mornings when I would wake up feeling like I could conquer the world—ready to climb that mountain. Then, out of nowhere, the anger would arise. I wonder how many other men and women can't let go of that anger. For me, it was looking at my kids and realizing all the time I lost with them. It was seeing them have to jump from one house to another, constantly moving their stuff because my Alcoholism made us unstable. We moved so many times in less than six months, all because of me.

BUT, again, you must constantly remind yourself that "things will be different moving forward." You have to wake up every day and try to be a better person. Process that anger with positive words that you're here, doing it, and getting better.

Anger is not a "bad" emotion if we process it in the right way. Anger tells us that something is wrong, that some boundaries have been crossed, and we react. But anger prevents us from living in the now and will rob us of tomorrow's now if we let it. I was angry at myself in my pursuit of Sobriety, but I had to process it naturally—not by drinking again, reverting back to old habits, or making the same mistakes. I needed to process it in a healthy way, and it all came back to forgiving myself.

What I want you to take away from this chapter is this: forgive yourself; forgive others. Sounds simple, yet so many people struggle with it. Years go by, and some take that struggle to the grave. But not you! You're going to look back one day and see this as trying time, but one that you needed to go through. You're going to reflect with gratitude that you got through it and are now victorious.

Process that anger, walk in true forgiveness, and you're on your way to breaking those generational strongholds and living a healthy life in Sobriety. Next time someone asks you, "Have you forgiven yourself?" and "Have you forgiven others?" you can look up with happiness and full confidence and say, "Yes." Forgiveness is the key! And this is how I did it.

I want to leave you with this:

Hurt people hurt people, but healed people heal people.

You're going to be a person that has healed, so you can help heal others.

Next, we're going to explore what this looks like, because I don't want you to be sober and still broken; I want you to be sober and healed.

Chapter 11

Hi, my name Is "Healing"

"We are all broken and wounded in this world. Some choose to grow strong at the broken places."
— Harold J. Duarte-Bernhardt

I wonder how many people could have fully healed in their recovery, if only they had just held on for one more day—if in that motel room, alone and defeated, they didn't let the shots and booze push them over the edge. Life is so hard. We've all made mistakes we're ashamed of; we all have shattered pieces of glass in our hearts that cut and make us bleed. And when that blood drips, we wonder if healing is even possible for our lives.

You're like me. I know you've thought about it. You even planned it out and visualized it in your head. You're fighting with yourself about why you should stay or go, going back and forth about whether or not your story should end this way. You're drowning, choking on your tears, the pain in your heart is unbearable. Those dark voices race through your mind. They speak relentlessly with apparent truth and authority, shooting thoughts at you like bullets. But behind every dark voice is a lie. They have no foundation and hold no light.

You sit there—in a tub, against the wall, in your room, outside—and you think, you reflect, you weep, you dig deep. And that pain, that past, that burden, that hurt, whatever it is, needs to heal the right way.

Sometimes, the way a person looks tells their story. When I do street ministry, my heart can't help but break for some people when I see them. Their dirty fingernails tell me they are still fighting for their lives. The blood stains on their shirt tell me they are still feeling. The bags under their eyes tell me they are still holding on. The smell of urine and the streets tells me they are doing what they can to survive. The smell of whiskey tells me they are trying to heal. I look at these people, hold them tight, and let them know that the pain they've been carrying is not theirs anymore.

What I've learned over the years is that we can get sober yet still be broken—we can recover yet still be damaged. And it doesn't get any better unless we learn to heal the right way. I want you to really think about what has been causing you to drink. What has been making you feel like you need to escape?

Too many people try to get sober without first healing what caused them to drink in the first place. Do you remember growing up and hearing, "Why are you crying?" "Just get over it," "Stop whining," or "Time will heal all wounds"? You probably heard all kinds of things that were supposed to make you feel better and guide you through rough times. But did they really help? Not allowing ourselves to express how we felt did much more damage than good. For years, we learned to bottle up all that hurt, not knowing how to process it in a healthy way. Now, we wonder why we struggle and feel how we feel. What are some areas in your life that need to heal? Not specific events from the past, but the underlying pain points that created those events. Remember, there is a root cause for everything in our lives—a deeper wound that drives us to do the things we do.

We have a lot of hurt people in the world—more specifically, we have a lot of drunk, hurt people in the world. And when we hurt, we bleed all over the people we love. We push away everyone that tries to get closer. Drowning in our hurt, we think if somehow we dilute that internal bleeding with alcohol, we won't feel or think anymore, but it's not true. When alcohol gets mixed in, we actually hurt and feel more, and it's a hurt with no end.

Starting now—right this moment—I want you to begin to heal the right way, the real way, for yourself and your family.

Get a journal and start writing. Be honest with yourself. Read some good books, move your body, pick up a hobby, or get outside in nature. See a therapist, a counselor, take some classes, read your Bible and pray. Do whatever you need to do to clear out your mind, body, and soul, so you can get to a place of healing.

We tend to think that if we ignore or don't talk about our pain, it will somehow disappear and cease to exist. But that's not the case. We have to spend time reflecting on where that hurt stems from and why it's been holding us down for so long. We have to be willing to dig and search for the sake of our Sobriety. We have to be willing to revisit our pain so we can process it, feel it, and begin to heal. I really want you to get this in your heart:

Healing is for you. It's for the deepest parts of your soul that nobody knows about. It's for a new life, better relationships, freedom, and peace of mind. Healing is for the promise of a clean and sober life—the life that you were meant to live.

When we cut ourselves physically, there are steps we must take to ensure we don't get an infection. First, we stop the bleeding, then put an ointment on it. Next, we determine how deep the cut is. Do we need stiches, or just a band-aid? We must understand the condition of our wounds before we can treat them. And when we take the proper steps, in time, we heal.

Right now, the cut is fresh—your wound is still open—so first, we need to stop the bleeding. What should we apply to it? How deep does it go? We need bandages when our wounds are still vulnerable. Whatever we do, we must be protective of our hearts and minds. In time, we too, will heal.

I wish I could tell you that healing happens overnight, but the truth is, healing is a complex process that takes time. Therefore, we must be very patient and gentle with ourselves. If we take our time, we'll heal the right way.

Many people give up because they don't see progress fast enough. They think it's impossible, so they stop trying altogether. Or perhaps they don't believe they even deserve it. Everyone deserves healing and a second chance. Hurt comes for us all; there's no way around it. From the moment we are born to the moment we die, we all experience hurt. Whether we brought it upon ourselves or it was brought unto us, everyone still deserves to heal. But what we do with that hurt—how we respond to that pain—is what makes all the difference in our lives.

Don't wait for that hurt to keep stacking up; let's start healing now in a healthy way.

People ask me all the time, "How do I know if I've really healed?" To this, I respond, "When we stop running from the hurt, stop allowing it to overshadow everything we love, and stop letting it bleed into everything we do." We know we are walking in the right direction when there's a peace in our hearts that cannot be explained. We've healed when that wound is no longer seen or felt by others—when we can begin to smile and live again. I want this for you.

Usually, when people take their lives, their hurt may end, but it gets passed down to others with even more intensity. If we don't deal with our own healing the right way, it will get passed down. Like water, hurt has to go somewhere.

So why not start the healing now? For your kids and grandkids and grandkids' grandkids. You can do this, friend. It's in you. You just need to get the process started. This chapter may even be the most important, because there really is no true Sobriety without healing and the freedom that brings. My hope is that you will take this chapter seriously and begin your own healing journey today.

Chapter 12

Hi, my name is "Functioning"

"If you're not moving away from a drink, then you're moving closer to it."

\- Recovery

I sat with a man in my office one day who had been dealing with drinking problems. One of the questions I asked him was, "Do you think you need help?" With a blank stare, he replied, "Well, my wife thinks I do."

I then said, "That's not what I asked you," and proceeded to ask the same question. This time, without hesitation, he said, "No, I don't think I have a problem with drinking." When I asked why that was, he said, "I go to work, I pay my bills, and I provide for my family. I drink with my friends on the weekends and don't see a problem with it."

This was me 13 years ago. I call these types of people "functioning alcoholics" and, in my experience, they are the hardest to reach. They may provide for their families, but they fail to see they have a problem. As long as they are not homeless and sleeping under a bridge, they don't think have a problem. There seems to be this assumption that alcoholics have already lost everything—no money, no job, no family, no direction. They're just lost and alone in their struggle. However, functioning alcoholics have it all (currently)—the money, job, and family. Their struggle is rather a silent and internal one. While their souls cry out for help, their lives don't display this same sense of urgency. They mask their problems with all the material things and the belief that "As long as I'm providing for my family, all is well." Under these conditions, they see no need for change. But in reality, the family is not well. They are walking on egg shells and are also suffering in silence. The material things don't matter; the truth is they want you well.

In my alcoholic days, as long as the bills were paid and my family had clothes on their backs and shoes on their feet, I drank whenever I wanted to. And I didn't want to hear what anyone had to say. Without missing a beat, I would go to the garage, crack open a beer, fire up my Harley, and ride off with a crisp bandana around my head. I'd hit up the nearest bar and that was my life for years—cruising, motorcycle rallies, bar hopping, girls, drinking, drugs, and trouble. No matter the consequences, I was okay with it. I simply was what I was—a drunk. In my eyes, as long as my family was taken care of, like that guy in my office, I saw no problem at all.

Being a functional alcoholic blinds us to our need for help, trapping us in the same old destructive patterns. Everyone can see it except ourselves, and the next thing you know, years have gone by.

This is what I learned as a functioning alcoholic myself. It's only a matter of time before what's functional becomes dysfunctional. Things will slowly start to unravel, to the point where we have no other choice but to change.

Eventually, my family left me, my money ran out, my home and cars and everything I once loved was gone. My reality had finally caught up to me. I found myself in a cold, dark, rehab room, alone and defeated. "Where did I lose control?" I would ask myself, even though everyone else saw it but me. The problem was it didn't happen over-night; it was years of self-denial in the making. And this is a scenario I see way too often.

If everyone is telling you that you need help, they are not saying it to be mean. Understand these are people who love and want the best for you. They are saying it because they see that the alcohol has consumed you and is con-trolling everything in your life. If you think you don't have a problem when everyone else does, you are the problem.

If you're late to work or showing up sick from a night out, this, my friend, is a problem. If you and your spouse fight constantly because of your drinking, this is definitely a problem. If your life is being altered in any way because of your drinking, there is obviously a problem.

Here's what I do know: All the warning signs were there, I just failed to see them—or rather, chose to ignore them. I didn't want to acknowledge that I had a problem, because that would mean I had to do something about it. Now, I sit with countless men monthly and it's the same old song and dance. They refuse to listen to what anyone says just because they see themselves taking care of business in their family.

Most drinkers know they have a problem but are too afraid of what their lives would look like without alcohol, as they've been doing it for a very long time. And my job as a recovery coach is to help them see past that. I also believe most functioning alcoholics like to feel needed and wanted. So as long as the work is getting done, the bills are getting paid, and the kids are getting what they need, they are satisfied and see no need for change.

The first question I always ask is, "Do you want help?" And I know what you're thinking. Why ask that question? Doesn't everyone want help? Unfortunately, the answer is no, not everyone does. They prefer their drinking no matter which road it takes them down.

Ask yourself these questions:

1. Do you see yourself as a functioning alcoholic?
2. Do you want help?
3. What steps will you take to get the help you need?

Last but not least, never be afraid to admit defeat! This was my issue for so long. My biker ego got the best of me, and I never wanted to admit that I was weak or needed help. That's a big NO when you come from the streets. But I learned early on that material things can be replaced, but family never can. Once Sasha took those kids and left, my world came crashing down before my eyes. My "functional" had now become dysfunctional, and some serious soul-searching needed to take place. Otherwise, my family was going to bury me.

But even then, I didn't think I was ready to get sober, and that was when I saw just how powerful Alcoholism was. You'd think that me losing my family and hitting the bottom of the barrel would sober me up, but that pain drove me to drink more. I just wanted to escape the nightmare that was my life. I was all alone, and this was the only way I knew how to get by.

I continued to drink until I almost lost my life, hitting an emotional wall to find that nobody could help me. All alone, I felt I was too far gone. Now, I was very dysfunctional. I came home to an empty cold house with no electricity or life, and I had no sense of direction about where to go or what to do. It wasn't until I woke up one morning with a somewhat clear mind after passing out the night before.

I knew something needed to change. There was no way I could keep living like I was living. I needed to introduce some structure back in my life, and I needed to get better—not just for my family, but for me. Once I made up my mind, I got a plan together and stuck with it. And that's when I began to see great things happen.

But first, I had to admit that everyone was right about me. And I finally saw how blind I had become—all the excuses I made repeatedly just to avoid getting help. Keep in mind, this didn't just go on for months; this went on for almost nine years. With every drink and excuse, I creeped closer and closer to being dysfunctional. And we never expect it to happen until it does.

So I ask you again, are you a functioning alcoholic? And do you want to get help to live a life in Sobriety? I hope the answer is yes because we need you!

Chapter 13

Hi, my name is "Responsibility"

"Stop validating your victim mentality. Shake off your self-defeating drama and embrace your innate ability to recover and achieve."
\- Steve Maraboli

"The devil made me do it." Does this sound familiar? Or "I was pressured." Here is my favorite: "I'm just going through life with the cards God dealt me. It's not my fault. I didn't ask for this life."

Okay, fair! But let me share something with you: we wake up every day with a choice. We all get to decide every day if we want to be better or worse. To be sober or an alcoholic? To blame or take responsibility? From what I've seen, almost everyone in the first stages of recovery chooses blame instead of responsibility. That's a hard one for many because it makes us step back and look at our lives for what they are, revealing what we really need to work on. And that work requires one hundred percent effort. It's not a one-time deal, but rather something we must pursue daily.

Sure, you can blame your lawyer for not getting you less time, but you committed the crime. Sure, you can blame your bad divorce for your overwhelming debt, but how much did you contribute to that divorce? You can even shake your fist at God, asserting that "if life were easier," you wouldn't be in a rehab home or prison. And the list goes on and on.

I certainly blamed God for my life growing up, and I even blamed my family. In fact, I practically blamed everyone else for my drinking over the years except myself. Passing the blame to others for my Alcoholism was easy, because it allowed me to take the focus off myself. And I excelled at playing the victim. However, once I sobered up and started thinking clearly again, I began to see that it was me alone who chose this road. It was me alone who made this mess out of my life. And for the first time in my life, I embraced responsibility.

If you do not take responsibility for your Alcoholism and every other decision in your life, you will remain stuck in victimhood, constantly pointing fingers at others. But nobody makes you drink; that choice is yours alone.

People who play the victim will never experience any real growth or peace in their lives. It's much easier to chop down someone else's tree than to water and nurture our own. And the drama of chopping, blaming, and self-pitying tends to appeal to us much more than assuming responsibility for the condition of our own tree. However, this drama will consume our lives and minds if we let it. It seems we have become an entitled society—we say what we want, when we want, and do as we please. But playing the victim will continue to hurt ourselves and others until we learn to heal and embrace responsibility. Perhaps this is also a learned behavior.

Taking responsibility for our own words, actions, and decisions will grant us so much more freedom than pretending to be innocent. Here are some ways to do it:

"Sorry" will be your favorite word for a while, and it's okay to say and process it daily. This simple word heals more than we know. It says "I own this" and "I'm going to work on getting better." But it only works if you mean it from your heart. People will know if it's what I like to call a "sloppy sorry," holding no weight, emotion, or humility. So when you say it, mean it!

I vividly remember having to look my loved ones in the eyes, get on my knees, and say I was sorry for what my Alcoholism had put them through all those years. I had to look at the mother of my children and say I was sorry for being the man I was. I would even apologize to people I ran into at the store for how I treated them in the past. And those apologies went a long way.

But what I learned about saying sorry is that we have to make sure we don't make those mistakes again; otherwise, it loses all meaning. My mom had a saying: "First time is an accident, second time is a habit."

Another thing we can do is put ourselves in a position to win, because, for so long, we put ourselves in a position to lose. This looks different for everyone, of course, but for me, it was going to church and working on the inner man. I went to classes and Bible studies, read books, and listened to positive things on YouTube and podcasts. I did what I had to do to see true change in my life for once. And I didn't want this just to be a phase that would pass; I wanted this to be a lifelong commitment to Sobriety. I wanted to be a better person and make up for how irresponsible I had been for so long. I wanted to take my life back—all those years I had lost—and begin to position myself for success.

When we embrace responsibility, we're essentially saying "Things need to change in my life." We're saying "I am responsible for my darkness and every decision I've made that's harmed others and myself." We're saying "I'm ready to stop the bleeding and have the life I was always meant to have." When we take our power back, we begin to crawl out of that pit and trade our victim mentalities for joy and peace.

Remember, every day, we get to wake up and make a choice, and those choices will shape our lives for better or worse. The thing about choices is they can make or break us. They can take years off our lives or maybe even add. But it's never too late to make better choices for our mental, spiritual, and physical well-being. In my opinion, that's the beauty of life: every day we get to open our eyes and make those good choices. I still want to work on being a better husband and father, no matter how old my kids are. I want to wake up every day and ask, "How can I be better than I was yesterday?" Because, one day, we won't get to make that choice anymore. One day, these bodies will die, but I want to die knowing I got up every day and made the best choices for my life, bettering myself and living the life I was always intended to live. Why? Because I chose to embrace responsibility. And I know you will do the same, friend. If no one told you today, I am so proud of you. You're learning and getting better every day.

Today, let's take full responsibility and put ourselves in a position to win. We all have to grow up and take ownership of our actions, letting go of childish thinking patterns that have kept us down for so long. It was hard for me to see and admit to everything I had done wrong, but once I did, I finally felt like I was growing up. And that was a good feeling to have.

Chapter 14

Hi, my name is "Trust"

"Our greatest weakness lies in giving up. The most certain way to succeed is to try just one more time."
—Thomas Edison

Let me ask you a question: where are you in life right now? In all areas of your life—mentally, physically, and spiritually? Take a moment to really think about this question, because it'll be important for this chapter.

I remember sitting on a park bench alone when I asked myself this almost 13 years ago. It was the first time I tasted what it felt like to be homeless for a night. "Why was I struggling like this?" I wondered. And "Why did I do it for so long?" I also recall asking myself, "What could I have done better with my family?"

Alcoholism robs us of many years, and the sad part is we typically don't recognize it until many years have passed. Our lifestyle was just normal to us. It was what we did cause it was all we knew.

I had been drinking for so long that it felt nearly impossible to visualize how a different life would look and feel for me—a new life of Sobriety. Feeling very discouraged, even afraid, I wondered, "What's left for me?" and "Could I really do this?" My false happiness had come from the bottle for so long that I wasn't sure if I could trust that happiness would come naturally.

And that's the purpose of this chapter: how can you trust? I know it seems scary—the unknown always does—like when long-term inmates get out of prison and normal life is scary for them. It's challenging because it's a new way of living.

Being Sober is no different. After years of drinking, normal life scares us—terrifies us, in fact. But we can do it.

Sobriety may look challenging from the current state we're in, but the more we just keep moving in that direction and trusting the process, the more normal and comfortable it will feel.

This is what I tell people: "You have been drinking for years"—twenty years or more for some—"you are not going to change overnight." It took almost three years for me to begin to see my purpose—to begin to see my life really start to come together. And my hope is that this chapter inspires you to have patience to see that through.

Here are three areas you really need to have trust in…

1. You need to trust the **PROCESS**.

I think one of the hardest parts about being told you have an illness is trusting the process. All the hospital visits, doctor appointments, and tests—it's definitely a waiting game. There are many challenging days, sleepless nights, and mental and emotional conflicts. And I know because I've been there.

But then I think about the Alcoholic who has lost everything—their job, home, car, friends, and family. Perhaps they sit cold and hungry in the streets, a jail cell, or rehab thinking, "How did I end up here?" and "Will I ever come out of this?"

Here's the truth: no matter how you feel, what you're going through, how hard things look right now, and whether the world is crumbling around you or the people you once trusted have turned their backs on you, **you have to trust the process**. Keep working, keep grinding, keep showing up, and keep going!

You won't see results right away, but sooner or later, you will see progress. And this requires trust. Don't give up too soon, as so many people who get caught up in their emotions and hardships do. You have to see past all this and keep going. It will all be worth it in the end. In our recovery class, I ask everyone to give me their "highs" and "lows" for the weekend. Highs are the awesome things, and lows are the challenging ones. It's a wonderful reminder that life is a balance; it's never just good and bad. Though, we must make sure to put more attention on our wins than our losses.

I look back at my life with huge gratitude that I kept moving—that I continued to press through even in my darkest hours, no matter how stuck or discouraged I felt. There were many times when I thought about giving up, but I knew I had come too far to quit. I had improved way too much to go back and had accomplished more than I ever thought I could. I truly believe that people can get to a point where they've seen so much bad, they don't even believe good is possible. They've seen so much darkness, they don't believe there is light. They've engaged in so much drinking, they don't believe they can be sober.

I'm so glad I stayed put, kept working, and trusted the process, because now, I am sober. I am also an author, pastor, counselor, traveling speaker, producer, scriptwriter, and grandpa. So many blessings have come into my life—blessing that I would have missed out on had I given up in the middle of the process. So believe me when I say "you have to trust the process," and know there is a beautiful outcome in store for you.

Right now, you may not see or feel it, but you must hang on—claw and fight if you have to. It will all be worth it, friend.

2.   You need to trust **YOURSELF.**

Let's be honest: sometimes, we can become our own worst enemies.

While this may be true, you have to learn to trust yourself again. Now, I'm not saying go and be around people you used to be around or return to the places you came out of, but you have more strength than you know. Don't be afraid of your triggers—study them, learn them, conquer them, and master them. If you fall, get back up. Don't be afraid to put the pieces of your life where they need to go.

If you're going to make it out of this, friend, you can't be afraid or timid in your recovery—you can't be afraid of you. You have to stay firm in your boundaries and know when to declare, "That's not me anymore." I knew some-one who, at one point, stayed home all the time because they couldn't trust themselves. In complete isolation, they became depressed, and it was a struggle every day. This is no way to live. Trust yourself again, and you'll live again. This is the only way to grow in your Sobriety.

The last point is for my people of faith…

3. You need to trust **GOD.**

If we are going to be people of faith, we must operate in this realm. We must have faith and trust in God that he will guide us, lead us, and keep his promises. In my new-found faith in Christ, I had to learn to trust him with my whole life. I had to dig deep in my heart and soul and say, "Okay, my life is now yours. Lead this thing and I will hold on for the ride."

Go to church, read the word, pray, and keep seeking and pressing through. Many people lose faith because they don't see things happening fast enough. They quit on God, they quit on life, and they quit on their recovery. I see too many people quit before the blessings come. Too many people quit before the breakthroughs. They give up before the promises are fulfilled and their purpose revealed.

Putting your trust in God will show you what you're made of. It'll show you what you need to work on and teach you many things. Whoever said "Life Is the greatest teacher" was correct. I certainly have found this to be true.

Now, you just need to be a student and learn. Don't quit before the lesson is complete.

Let's read this again:

Trust the process, trust yourself, and trust God.

Trust the promises in your life, trust the purpose for your life, and trust that the outcome is on its way. It will all be worth it.

Chapter

15

Hi, my name Is
"Different"

"The person who follows the crowd will usually go no further than the crowd. The person who walks alone is likely to find himself in places no one has ever seen before." – Albert Einstein

Things change. Seasons come and go. That's life. Nothing will stay the same. So rather than asking if we have changed over our lives, we should ask ourselves how have we changed. How have we changed in the past seasons and how can we change in the upcoming seasons?

Many people want to be different but don't understand the work that comes with it. Different requires drastic change in our lives, and drastic change calls for drastic action and effort. It also requires growing up and having thick skin. In this chapter, we will talk about what that looks like for you. But first, keep this in mind:

Don't be afraid of being different. Be afraid of being like everyone else.

Now, I don't say this to bash our friends, but how many of you have friends your age that are still doing the same things? They're in the same scene with the same talks, same attitude, same patterns, same troubles—all the same!

I bet we all can if we think about it. Again, our friends are not bad people, and we are not better than them. But we are different. The question is: how different do we want to be?

You see, when I sobered up, I wanted to be different. And I needed to look through a different lens. I also needed to know moving forward that my life would never be the same as yesterday. I had flirted with darkness for too long and opened too many doors I wish I'd never opened. When I started to get sober, what I felt was real. And for once in my life, I felt proud of who I was becoming. I wanted to continue down this path and be different in my Sobriety—not just a sober version of my old self.

I didn't want to be like everyone else, and I definitely didn't want to be trapped in my family's generational strongholds. I wanted to be different in how I handled situations, how I saw others and myself—I just wanted to be different In general.

Consider this: we only get one shot at this life. Once it's over, it's over. No redoes. No coming back. Life is too short to stay the same, thinking "I should've done this" or "I should've done that." Now is the time to be different and start living the life you were meant to live—not a life consumed by alcohol.

What I learned early on was if I was going to be different, there were three areas I needed to focus on:

1. Commitment

This is essential if we really want to see lasting change in our lives. The problem is, today we live in a feel-good society—as long as we feel good, we'll stay committed. But any person who's been married long enough knows that's not how it works. A long-term healthy marriage takes hard work from both sides, and there are certainly times that don't feel good. But we make it work because we are committed in our love for each other. Nowadays, however, most people will drop everything the moment it doesn't feel good. If you're going to base your Sobriety on feelings—well, good luck with that. Let me know how it works out for you.

If we are going to see change in our lives when it comes to Sobriety, we must be COMMITTED. And we must be driven by our goals rather than our emotions.

As I type this, I am exhausted. It's been a long, emotional week, and I am ready to lay down and spend time with my son. Yet, here I am working on this chapter, so I can get this book out to the world. Why? Because I am committed to what I am doing and driven by the positive impact I could have on people's lives.

Here's what sets us apart from the rest: while people are in their feelings, making excuses for the way they're living their lives, we are staying committed, even when it gets challenging and uncomfortable. Even when we get tired, we are maintaining razor-sharp focus. And we must make this a part of our DNA if we want to be different and create lasting change.

What areas of your life do you need to stay committed to? Remember, your emotions should not dictate your commitments, so don't allow them to steer you off track. Feelings will always come and go, but your commitments should be strong.

Think of it this way: you're fishing on a commercial boat in the sea, when, out of nowhere, a storm brews and the waves begin to rock the boat aggressively. The captain now has a choice—either stay put and get lost at sea or move the boat closer to land for a fighting chance at survival. No matter how bad it looks—how much of a beating the boat is taking—he decides to get his crew to safety, committing to the course whether he feels good or not.

This must be you in this stage of your life. No matter what Alcoholism has taken from you, how difficult the path looks, or how scared or uncomfortable you feel, you must stay the course. You must stay committed.

On the other side of commitment is:

2. Discipline

Understand this about commitment and discipline: **Commitment is the *decision*. Discipline is the *execution*.** In Chapter 4, we looked at what areas we need to be disciplined in. Here, we are going to examine discipline in greater detail.

When we set goals for ourselves, we need commitment and discipline to achieve them. And it takes a lot of work in the beginning, because our drinking has made us very undisciplined.

You're supposed to be home by 6 pm for dinner? No way. "One more drink" turns into four and now its 8 pm and you're in a lot of trouble. Thought you could drive yourself home from the bar? Now you're in jail for a DWI, or worse, in prison for killing someone. You're married and it's guys' night? Instead of saying no to the lady who bought you a drink, you said yes to her bed and are now divorced after twenty years of marriage. Planned on staying at the bar for only an hour or two? Instead you shut it down and are now late for work the next morning—perhaps even fired. Are you getting the picture? Alcoholism made your life so undisciplined. In your Sobriety, or in any change you want to make in life, you must be disciplined after you make the commitment to change.

This will look different for everyone, of course. For me, it was returning to school and ensuring I studied when I was supposed to. It was also finding a job and working hard to support my family.

This level of discipline is required to execute our goal of Sobriety. It says "I choose to stand out above the rest in everything I do, whatever that looks like." And it's an internal process. It's how goals are realized and winners are made.

The last part will make us or break us:

3. Confidence

Commitment is the decision, discipline is the execution, but confidence is a gift you give yourself. And it's a gift you must give yourself daily, because it takes a steady belief in yourself to maintain your commitments and accomplish the goals you've set into motion. See the small wins—no matter how small—as a gift, and allow them to boost your confidence.

For example, when I started to sober up, I had no job or bank account. Getting a job after being out of work for almost four months was a win for me. Then after I got my job, I got my bank account. No matter how small it might've looked to others, those wins gave me the confidence I needed to turn my life around. I stayed committed and disciplined throughout the process, because I was finally thinking clearly for once in my life and all these small changes gave me momentum.

In the recovery process, I believe people lack confidence more than ever. They have been drinking for so long, they don't see change as even possible. They have been "bad" for so long, they don't believe good is even within their reach. They don't believe things can change at this point, and they don't believe they deserve a better life. In short, they lack the confidence they need.

But I want things to be different for you. I want you to have confidence in yourself and your ability to get sober. Have confidence that things will get better for you no matter how difficult the circumstances are right now. Remember to take stock of all the small wins in your life, because every small win is a new goal met. And this should build your confidence in life and Sobriety. No matter what season you are in, know that you will come out of it.

The key is believing you deserve a great life, which starts with believing you deserve a second chance. Do this, and you will come out stronger and better than ever. Commit to getting up every day and moving even when you don't feel like moving—stay the course even when you feel like giving up. Today, give yourself the gift of confidence.

Different!—that's what we need to be, and I want you to embrace it.

When I found my calling, I ran with it and am still running today. At 42, I am still dreaming and believing in great things for my life in Sobriety. So I write, I speak, I travel, and more. One of my greatest joys is traveling and sharing my story at events and churches—how I became sober and got a second chance at life. My life is certainly not perfect, but I now believe it's for a purpose. And so is yours! But you have to be okay with being different and utilizing your unique gifts in life. You also must be ready for the talk that being different brings.

Living with purpose and meaning in your life will always come with unfair criticism.

But you must not allow that to discourage you. Run with it! Embrace it! Be different and stand out. There will always be people who try to put you in a box. The haters, snakes, and backstabbers—they will respect you in public but disrespect you in private. What I learned is that people don't fight us as individuals; they fight the gift in us, because it looks different than theirs. They fight our calling, because they fail to follow their own.

Whatever the case may be, keep making strides. Don't let the noise make you afraid of being different. Make commitments, stay disciplined, and be confident in your small wins. If you want to be different—to have a new life in Sobriety—these three pieces are essential.

Chapter 16

Hi, my name is "New"

> *"Every sunset is an opportunity to reset. Every sunrise begins with new eyes."*
>
> - Richie Norton

I always wondered why so many people would dwell on the past until I got my own. I also wondered why so many people resisted change until I did the same.

I think it's because we like to be comfortable. Even if our pasts were painful, they're familiar. New things require us to step out of our comfort zones. That's why taking a new job, moving to a new state, or even making new friends can be challenging. The same applies to getting sober. Everything in your life needs to be NEW.

If you're still drinking, it's probably because the old is still rubbing against the new. You haven't learned to let go, so the old lingers in the corner, just waiting for the right time to strike. And it always seems to catch us at our weakest moment—moments when it thinks we need it—which is why we must remain cautious.

Old things must die for new things to be birthed. Start thinking about all the old things that have been driving you towards alcohol—the things you just can't seem to let go of. I hear a lot of people say, "My new life will be boring," or "What am I going to do for fun now?" This kind of thinking already sets you up for failure. Sobriety requires a new attitude, because what you think and say is what you're going to feel and believe, my friend.

So here are three areas of change we need to focus on:

1. New Habits

Let's say you're at a company function and everyone's got a beer in their hand. Don't be ashamed of drinking water or sparkling water. Don't even be ashamed of leaving before the party starts. Embracing your new habits is something you not only need to be okay with—it's something you should feel proud of! You may have been the life of the party months ago—the first to dance on the table and make everyone laugh—but today you're a new person with new habits. The problem is that we tend to care what people may say or think.

But remember, it's okay to be different and stand out. I can promise you this: those people at your company party are trying to find themselves in alcohol as well. And you're a light to people more than you know in your Sobriety. When they are ready to sober up or make a change in their life, who are they going to come to? You! Because you clearly know what it takes and can be that encouraging voice for them when they need it.

But let's take it a step further: don't be ashamed around your family in your new habits. From my experience, the pushback will be greater with those close to you. Since they have known you their whole life, this new habit is completely foreign to them. I remember one time, one of my uncles came up to me and said "So you're really serious about this Sobriety thing?" Seeing me walk around with a coffee in my hand instead of a beer came as quite a shock to those who've known me the longest. It was also new to everyone that once the football game or function ended, I was getting ready to go home instead of the store for another twenty pack. But these were my new habits, and I was okay with it.

Now, look what happened: I made it! We made it. Alcoholism did not care about us and death was knocking on our door. It wanted to swallow every bit of our souls much sooner than we were ready. But here we are, friend, living and breathing. While the majority of people seek to find themselves in all the wrong places, we have found it in Sobriety. We are slowly healing from all the damage that's been done to our bodies and lives. If I had never stopped drinking, I would not be here writing this book today. My body would have given out and shut down long ago. I would have been another number in my family line's generational Alcoholism.

Let me ask you this: what are you going to do with the second chance you have been given in life? Really pause to consider this, because so many people don't get that second chance. Are we lucky? No. We just decided to change sooner. We got tired, felt helpless, and knew deep down that something needed to change before it was too late. And it all started with forming new habits.

The next thing I want you to focus on and enjoy is your:

2. New lifestyle

This can be tricky for many, especially those who came from the streets. Once removed from a way of life we were so used to, it can be difficult to know how to feel. From substituting lemonade tea for 40's with our friends, to trading late nights out with the guys for movie nights at home and bed by 9 pm—okay, that last part was for me (I do love my sleep)—our lifestyle will look completely different in Sobriety.

And it's important to fall in love with your new lifestyle. It doesn't make you lame or weak; it just means your life is new and different. You may have to find new hobbies and that's okay. With a new lifestyle comes new surroundings and typically new friends. And this is the challenge for many, because they love their old surroundings and friends.

Remember, you have to let go of the old to make way for the new. You have to release your old self to find peace and fulfillment in your new self. You have to fall in love with the person you're becoming—the person you've always dreamed of or perhaps never even imagined.

Your lifestyle is something that people will simply have to get used to, and those that love and support you will embrace it. Those that don't probably don't need to be in your life, and in time you will find out who those people are. Today, I am very thankful for the support system I've had for the last 13 years of Sobriety. My primary support system is my beautiful wife and wonderful kids. They have been with me since day one. Despite all the hard times we've been through, I continue to have their support. I am also extremely grateful for the men God puts on my path and the strength and love they have for me. Find those good friends that will support you on the bad days, not just the good.

The last point I want to discuss is your:

3. New Thinking

One of the main things I teach people is that our thinking has to change. We have to eliminate negative thinking and self-talk, because it's a breeding ground for wanting to drink again.

This negativity, if left unchecked, will drag you back to your old habits and lifestyle. Your new thinking has to be optimistic and determined, with the belief that, "No matter how things look right now, I am going to get through this! No matter how long drinking has been a part of my life, I can make a turnaround!"

I remember sitting in my backyard one day, about to finish a 20 pack and thinking, "This is just my life; this is who I am." Even if I wanted to quit drinking, I wasn't sure I even had the willpower to do so. Then, I had another negative thought: "I am not meant to be somebody in this life. I have no purpose."

The purpose part is what hit me the most. To wake up and feel like you have no purpose—like you're a waste space—can be the worst feeling in the world. You have no hope in life.

When I first sobered up, I would say things like, "Life is going to be real boring on Sundays when I watch football without a beer," and, "Going out to eat is going to be real dry without a cold one." Do you see what was happening? I started to believe the lies I was feeding myself.

But now, I can assure you that it's the opposite. A sober life is rewarding. Speak positive and uplifting words over your Sobriety, and I promise, you will come to experience the same. Adopt a new mindset, a new way of thinking, and, most importantly, a new inner voice.

When I started to sober up, it also helped that I started to think and see things more clearly, and so will you. First, you have to believe you have a purpose in life; and second, you have to believe Sobriety is a long-term game (not a one-month game). You also must cultivate a unstoppable inner voice, and it must roar like a lion every day. The lion's roar is meant for one thing: to scare its enemy—to let them know that if they get any closer, you will fight. That roar within you must be bigger than your negative talk; otherwise, you will never get anywhere.

I made my mind up a long time ago: if I was really going to get sober, everything in my life had to change—from my habits, to my lifestyle, to my thinking. And we cannot embrace Sobriety until we start getting these things in order.

Change these three things and you will change your life. It won't happen overnight, but it must be done. Just know that all things are new, all things are possible, and all things can have fresh meaning and purpose in your life. The rest is up to you! If no one told you today, I am so proud of you!

Chapter 17

Hi, my name is "You"

"Rest and self-care are so important. When you take time to replenish your spirit, it allows you to serve from the overflow. You cannot serve from an empty vessel." - Eleanor Brown

First of all, I want you to understand that I get you! I know how you think, how you operate, how you feel, and what you're going through right now, because I was exactly where you were. I lost everything I loved and knew, so I know what it's like to be without, to struggle, to fight, and to just try to stay afloat. But I also know how to survive and make it through.

If you're going to have any fighting chance in Sobriety, you need to do this for **YOU**. That's right, for you and no one else. I've heard countless people say they were doing it for their spouse, parents, or family. But when I hear that I know that they don't truly want it. And if they don't want it for themselves, all other motives will eventually fall short.

For years, that devil lurked at my door, just waiting for the right time to knock. I could practically hear him breathing and see him pressing up against it with his crafty smirk. Sometimes, I could hear him walk away, but he was always lingering nearby, keeping close watch on my door to see if the time was right. Then, one day, I finally heard a knock. I let the devil in and knew I had now invited hell into my heart—a darkness like never before. Since then, I was stuck in a season of cloudiness and harsh storms. And it was a season I brought on myself. Like so many others , I opened a door that should have stayed shut, and I was now knee-deep in this puddle of tar called Alcoholism. I tried to get out, but the devil left his demons behind to hold me down. It was like I was a hostage within my own soul, and it was the worst feeling in the world—when you want to get out but can't. Those demons had a tight grip and I suffered in silence for a long time. So once I finally broke free, I ran very far away. But that dark residue still lingered, so my mind, heart, and spirit had to go through what I call a "Soul Searching Detox."

That's why it's so important that your Sobriety be just for you. It's much deeper than what it appears. It takes a deep inner drive and desire to change—to strip away the darkness and let in the light—and that depth can only come from inside you. We tend to think that all we need to do is stop drinking. No, friend, there are a lot of shattered pieces in our lives that we need to put back together. And we have to find ourselves all over again to do it. Cleansing our body requires cleansing our heart, mind, and spirit. Our whole being goes through a detox like never before. We get the toxins out—the demons that have held us down for too long—and establish a new identity independent of alcohol.

I tend to think of it like this: I love Saunas; they come with a lot of health benefits and are very therapeutic for me. As my body temperature rises, I sweat, I detox. With each drop of sweat that drips from my brow, more and more toxins are pushed out of my body—all the things that don't need to be there.

Again, doing this on a soul level is much deeper than we think, and it requires that you do it for yourself.

I once looked somebody in their tired eyes, the scent of liquor coming through their pores, and told them, "You need to get better for you. You need to fight for you. You need to get sober for you. It's not selfish—it's right! If you're not okay, no one else can make you okay, because no one will value your life more than you. And nobody knows you better than you. Only you know who and what you need and don't need."

I hear many people say, "I can't go to a 6-month program. My family needs me to provide for them." But my question is, "What about you? Who takes care of you?" If you don't take care of yourself, you'll never be truly capable of taking care of others. And you can't expect anyone else to take care of you.

When will you start caring for yourself emotionally, mentality and physically? Because you can't be sober and still toxic. And you can't expect all the toxins to go away just because you stopped drinking. There are emotional, mental, and spiritual toxins as well. And you need a daily detox to deal with these.

Self-care will look very different for everyone because we all come from different backgrounds, with a variety of old habits and learned behaviors. We're also all different when it comes to our experience with Alcoholism. Some of us went through it married, while others divorced or single. All of us are unique, but I want to touch on three things that have helped me over the years, so hopefully they will help you.

1. Make a plan and ask the right questions.

Sounds simple, though it's very effective. What do you need to work on? Have you been a certain way your whole life? What does self-care look like for you? What are your gifts and talents? What's your stress reliever? What are your dreams? What makes you smile? What makes you happy? You have been buried in Alcoholism for so long, you've lost touch with the real you. But you can find yourself again by starting with a plan and asking the right questions.

Right now, I am in my element. I am in my place of peace. I am writing this book in a coffee shop in Colorado. I've been here for 4 hours already and will continue to write and dream. Good coffee shops are my place of relaxation, planning, and thinking. For years, I sat on a bar stool and destroyed every bit of my being. Now, I sit in a cafe, healing every part of me as I live and write. I mean, who doesn't like a good cup of coffee or tea?

2. Don't be afraid of learning new things, of feeling and seeing through a different lens.

We have been wired a certain way for years—from how we were raised to how we raise our kids, from how we handled money to how we respond to things in life, even from how we feel to how we love others. I hate to break it to you, but as you sober up, you will start to get in touch with your feelings.

Why? Because that's the real you—the caring, loving person that feels.

I think we can all relate to shedding a tear or two when we see a sad movie. Now, however, after 13 years of Sobriety, I cry at every sad and happy scene. If I could insert a laughing emoji, it would be here. It's just a movie, for crying out loud. Why am I crying all the time? Why do I cry when I hear that someone made it out of the pits of Alcoholism?

Because I've realized that I don't need to be afraid of feeling. For so long, I had completely shut myself off from feeling. Now that I'm sober, I feel everything. I see through a different lens and am okay with learning new things about myself. And you need to be okay with it too, my friend. When you start working on yourself, you will see a different person in the mirror—one who feels and sees things differently. You will see through a lens not stained with Alcoholism, but clear with Sobriety. You will see the world for what it is and your purpose for what it can be. Everything looks different when you're sober.

Embrace that new perspective of your outer and inner world. It's okay to learn about you again.

The last one is short but simple:

3. Keep working through.

As you detox daily, the toxins will continue to come out. Let them take their course and fill yourself with good things in their place. There will certainly be moments when you think, "I didn't see that coming," or "This is an entirely different kind of feeling." Just keep working and keep getting better for YOU. Keep setting goals for you, dreaming for you, and staying sober for you. When you're better inside, everyone else will be too.

Doing Sobriety for yourself holds much more weight, because it's an investment that nobody else can make for you. When it's your skin in the game, you will protect that Sobriety more than anyone else. And as you get up every day and put in work, it will mean more to you.

If you take one thing away from this chapter, let it be this:

When it's all said and done, you will have done this for YOU! You will be sober for you! And that's the greatest feeling ever. Now go! Work on and take care of YOU!

Chapter 18

Hi, my name is "Apply"

"No matter how hard the past is, you can always begin again." - Buddha

Here we are! Last Chapter of the book, I hope it challenged you and made you think, but most importantly, I hope it inspired you. I'm so thankful I could accompany you on this journey of Sobriety. If we're honest, I'm sure we can all admit to not thinking we'd make it. But we did and now here we are.

These are the questions you must ask yourself now: What am I going to do with all that I've learned from this book? What do I need to do to continue to live a life of Sobriety and break those generational strongholds for my family?

One of the most discouraging things is when you see people return from a year of rehab and go right back to drinking again. What happened? Did they get lazy? Are they easily tempted?

No. What happened is they never applied what they learned.

We all have triggers, and we all feel tempted from time to time. But what tools have we acquired to resist these triggers? We have to utilize these tools. Anyone can read a book like this and think it was a good read, but never take any action—never take the necessary steps to break those generational strongholds and pave a new path. Many simply continue with to stumble through life in their old ways.

Have you heard the saying, "Take it one day at a time"? That's the worst advice for someone who's trying to get sober. One day sober is like the worst feeling ever. It's our insides buzzing, our mind racing, the feeling of dying inside with each passing minute. But you have to keep going and applying what you've learned. Don't take it one day at a time, take it one lesson at a time.

Think of it this way: we all love a great mechanic. They analyze your car to see why it's making that noise, and usually they know how to fix it. But even a good mechanic will tell you that, every now and then, they also get stuck with a problem they can't solve. What do they do in these moments? Give up? No! They are determined to find the problem and fix it. They read a manual or look it up on YouTube. They find the problem and **APPLY** what they've learned. And thank goodness they do, because now your car is fixed and back on the road. You have a happy customer and a happy mechanic.

It's always easier to give up when a problem arises, because it takes courage to rise above, find a solution, and apply what we learn. But we must be willing to face these challenges if we want to succeed in our recovery. We have everything we need to work on our lives; we just need to be willing to apply.

I also want to leave you with this: never stop learning. Always look for ways to make yourself sharper in your mind and Sobriety, but you have to make sure you master the things you have learned first before moving on to new things. Remember, one lesson at a time.

I always tell people to pay attention to the not-so-sharp areas in their lives. And once they identify one, learn about it and sharpen it. For example, I once had a guy who always seemed to break down during the weekends. He would be fine for the week, then cave when the weekend hit. Weekends were always his breeding ground for drinking. It was simply a habit he couldn't seem to get out of. So I advised him to change up his weekend routine by doing something else out of the norm. He started going fishing, golfing, and dirt bike riding, and eventually, he began to realize that he didn't need to drink anymore. Of course, he also had some accountability, but the pivotal step was identifying what was taking him backwards. Now, he is well on his way to a life of Sobriety.

Study what you need to and apply.

I also knew a guy who wouldn't guard his heart in relationships, so every time he'd meet a girl, he would relapse. So we identified some things, and he applied some new affirmations to his learning, such as "Build a strong foundation" and "Guard my heart In Sobriety." He needed to work on himself for a while before he could start dating again. He needed to mend his own heart before he could give it away. And he did this by making sure to ask all the right questions. Once he started applying what he learned, change followed. What helped was taking his mind off Sobriety and setting his heart on love. Though, if he let his guard down, he'd end up in a relationship with someone who drank and be right back to drinking himself.

The lesson here is that we can't compromise our Sobriety for love, no matter how lonely we get. If they drink, it is extremely likely we'll eventually go down that road again, which never ends well.

The point that I want to make here is this: We can read all the books, listen to all the podcasts, and take all the classes on Sobriety that we want. But unless we start applying what we have learned, we will never see change. A year will go by and our lives won't look any different. The fact that I am 13 years sober and clean today is not an accident; it's because I applied what I learned, knew, and leaned into with my faith daily. And I continue to do this to this day, because I can't afford to take any days off in my Sobriety.

On that note, I leave you with this: I am your biggest fan all the way from New Mexico. The truth is I am nobody special. God has just given me a voice and I want to use it the best way I can. Everyone is searching, but most people are searching in the wrong places. I want to help as many people as possible by inspiring hope and change in their lives. Though, if I could help just one person out, it was all worth it.

We must break the silence of Alcoholism, getting ourselves and families back. But most importantly, we must break every generational stronghold that has been passed down through our lineage for years. I love you, friend, and I am rooting for you, because I want you to make it and succeed in life. If you ever feel like giving up or feel like there's no one out there who cares about you, please know that I care. I am supporting you every step of the way—until you cross that finish line of Sobriety! You are made for great things, and you have a purpose. Never lose sight of who you really are. It's not how we start this life; it's how we finish, and you are going to finish strong! I believe in you, just believe in yourself. Enjoy your new life in Sobriety with passion and purpose!

About the Author

Anthony Torres was born in Altus, Ok. He grew up in Las Cruces, NM, and now resides in Alamogordo, NM with his wife, Sasha Torres. He is the father of 4 wonderful kids and a proud Grandpa. He is the Pastor of MountianVIEW Church, a Church that is outreach driven to REACH1 in its community, he also the founder of "New Life Recovery." His heart is in seeing people set free from addictions.

Connect with him on social media:
Facebook: @reach1forHOPE
Instagram: @author.anthony.t

If you'd like to write Anthony you can send letters to MountianVIEW Church, 1300 Cuba Ave Alamogordo, NM 88310: Attention Anthony Torres. Or you can email him at Anthony@mvagalamo.com

CHECK OUT OTHER BOOKS FROM THE AUTHOR:

AWARD WINNING BOOK

"Letters to my People"

Thoughts of a Recovering Addict.

www.recoveredaddict21.com or on Amazon

GET YOUR COPY TODAY!

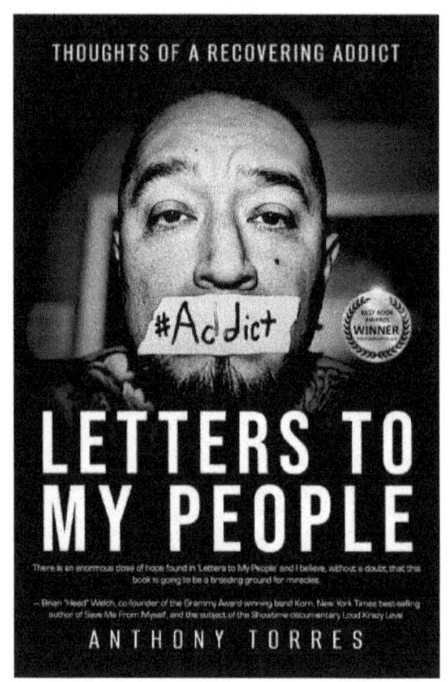

"Devotions to my People"
31 Days to Boost your Devotion Life in Recovery
www.recoveredaddict21.com or on Amazon
GET YOUR COPY TODAY!

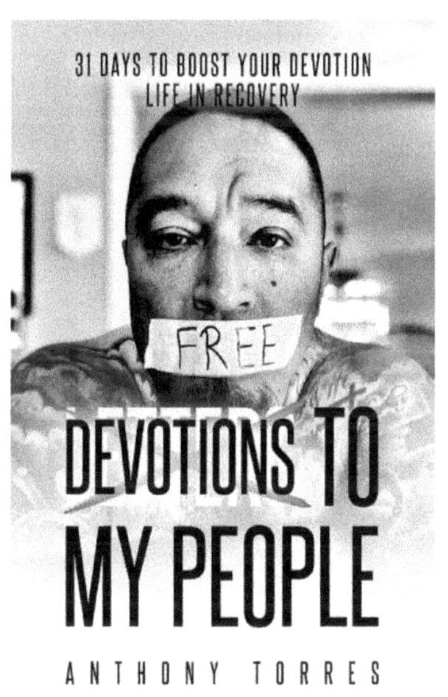

9 798886 917360 7